DANCING

WITH THE

SCARS

Finding hope when life hurts.

BARRY STAGNER

www.xulonpress.com

To all who long to dance again

You have turned my mourning into joyful dancing.
You have taken away my clothes of mourning
and clothed me with joy.

— PSALM 30:11 (NLT)

Table of Contents

Preface

Having looked into the eyes of individuals, couples, and families from across my desk for many years, having heard their stories, seen their joys and sorrows, and listened to their struggles and disappointments, it's easy to conclude that there's an ebb and flow to life that everyone experiences to some degree. Good times and bad times, feast and famine, joy and sorrow—all are the life experiences of everyone, no matter their station or status in life.

I don't know that I can say that I've heard or seen it all, but I would be comfortable in saying that there isn't much that I haven't heard or had to deal with in my years in ministry. I can also say with full confidence, however, that there is one thing that I've seen in the eyes of some that has left me feeling helpless, even as someone who has spent my life trying to encourage and strengthen others while they journey through that ebb and flow. What is the "one thing"? Hopelessness. There are many roads that lead there, but there is only one road out, and that is to have hope renewed or restored.

Time can lessen the pain of traumatic life events, but time can't cure hopelessness. Closure in a broken relationship can allow someone to move on to the next season of life, but hopelessness is already a closed door that doesn't need closure. Hopelessness needs hope.

This is my desire for the reader of *Dancing with the Scars*: that anyone, no matter what road they may have taken to arrive there, might learn how to restore hope when life hurts—that hearts and minds would mend and begin to experience hope, joy, and peace once again. I know that it's possible, because with God nothing is impossible! Yet sometimes we forget, as do others around us, that restoring hope isn't an instantaneous thing. It takes time, and it requires taking risks and even unwanted steps at times. But hope can be found again! It *can* be restored, no matter what may have caused it to be lost in the first place.

Hope doesn't return without help, and the power required to restore hope comes from *without* and not from within. People who have been traumatized by life are often pointed to their inner selves or asked to tap into the strength within themselves. Such requests are like dropping a bucket down an empty well trying to draw up water. The great "hope restorer" is none other than God himself, a source of power outside of ourselves, who alone has the capacity to do things in the hearts, minds, and emotions of people whom life has wounded terribly.

I've compiled ten chapters that deal with some common life events that can bring about hopelessness, and the topics in each chapter are very specific and by no means exhaustive. This isn't a book of statistics or medical causes and cures, but it is a book that points you to the Worker of Miracles—the One who can turn "mourning into dancing"; the One who can restore the years that have been eaten away with hopelessness, and who can not only help you to live life again but to do so with joy!

One last thing before your "dance lesson" begins. Certain chapters may not apply to your own personal life experience, but I can assure you that every chapter deals with an issue that someone you know is facing. So keep reading, and be equipped to help others to learn to dance with their scars even though theirs may be different from yours.

As Moses was commanded by God to speak over Israel, may I speak the same over you as you continue your journey in search of restored hope and joy:

The Lord bless you and keep you;
The Lord make His face shine upon you,
And be gracious to you;
The Lord lift up His countenance upon you,
And give you peace.

— NUMBERS 6:24-26 (NKJV)

Blessings to you as you begin a new season of life: Dancing with the Scars!

1

Life Happens

I f there are any aspects of life from which we would all love to be exempted, they are pain, sorrow, and suffering. Yet even knowing that it's impossible to avoid these doesn't lessen the agony or the impact when they come into our lives. Some of the age-old questions many have pondered are: Why does God allow suffering? Why do children die? Why do young moms get cancer? Why are innocent dads killed by drunk drivers? Why do famines and plagues sweep over mankind at times? The list is almost endless of things that we view as intrusions upon a rich and full existence.

The fact is, life happens. Most of us understand and believe that sin has brought into this world all the things that trouble us most, particularly concerning pain, sorrow, and suffering. Bible-believing Christians acknowledge the fact that man himself introduced sin into this world. Sin carries with it almost innumerable consequences and companions, but even though we understand and acknowledge this, it doesn't lessen the pain when these things invade our own lives.

A crucial starting point that we must acknowledge in this process of learning to "Dance with the Scars"— scars that most of us will accumulate during our lifetimes—is simply this: There has to *be* a starting point! There *must* be a place where we begin the process of healing and realize that those critical elements of hope, joy, and peace can still be ours. We realize that we can still have the ability to smile and even laugh in spite of the fact that trauma or tragedy has been forced into our life experience.

So what can we do when life happens? I'm talking about life in a fallen and sin-filled world where the consequences of sin intrude upon one's personal life in their untimely and uninvited ways. How do we handle those "Why, God?" events that life brings? Things that don't make sense; things that we, as finite, thinking human beings, realize could have been avoided, averted, or resolved, and yet the trauma, pain, and sorrow came anyway. Can we really just say flippantly to ourselves and to others, "Well, life happens"? Hardly! The goal of this chapter is to help you to realize that when life brings things along that have the capability of stopping your life in its tracks and scarring you for the rest of your life, there has to be a point where we finally say, "I am going to begin life again."

We'll talk about specifics in the coming chapters, but very simply, we all know that there are two points that are common to any race, whether it be cars or motorcycles, runners or swimmers: there's always a starting line and a finish line. The whole race will have to be run. They might consist of different distances, depending on the type of race, but they all begin at the same place.

The very same thing is true for those trying to get through a life that has been forever altered. The race may be longer for some than for others, but each of us must still begin at the starting line. In life, you can't begin in the middle of the race, and you can't end before the finish line if hope, joy, and peace are going to return with their companions of laughter and purpose for your life. This is important, because we often allow our minds to go down the path of "Why me?" *Why did my prayer for healing not give me the answer I wanted, and yet so-and-so won their battle with cancer? Why did the drunk driver hit the wonderful person that I loved instead of hitting some evil person?* Or even, *Why did the drunk driver survive and my loved one was killed or maimed? Why was my childhood brutal or abusive? Why did divorce come? Why was I betrayed?* All of these questions are normal and natural, and they demand answers, but any answer seems unacceptable to our hearts and minds—and still, life continues, and so must you.

What is the starting line for you? For most, if not all, whom life has wounded deeply, it begins here:

Recognize that you will have to move forward
with unanswered questions.

The truth is that those unanswered "whys" are where many, wounded by life, tragically spend the rest of their days. They never even make it to the starting line. As in any race, the starting line might be drawn on the ground or marked with a flag or banner, but the racer must approach the line with questions in his/her own mind about the race in which he/she is about to engage. You may have unanswered questions too. The runner may wonder if he will win, or if that recent injury will hamper his performance. The racer might be concerned about a crash and the swimmer, endurance, but they still enter the race. So, too, must you! You may not want to, you certainly won't feel like it, but when a sufficient amount of time has passed, everyone wounded by life must try to get back into the race, recognizing that they will have to move forward with many unanswered questions. The big question is: *How?*

I have often reminded Christians that our mind-set in life is to be "future first" thinkers. Paul wrote in 1 Thessalonians 4:13 to those concerned about the loss of their loved ones:

> *But I do not want you to be ignorant, brethren,*
> *concerning those who have fallen asleep, lest you*
> *sorrow as others who have no hope.* (NKJV)

Note that Paul didn't say, "Because you are going to Heaven you should have no sorrow," but rather he said that because we are going to Heaven, we sorrow, yet with hope. The fact is, dear friend, there are some life events that we will never get over but that we are going to have to get through. We sorrow—and we hope. Our hope is that when life happens and hurts us at times, the future for the Christian is Heaven. This life is not all there is. This isn't trite, nor is it merely a quaint saying that we throw out when pain and sorrow infringe upon our lives. It's an age-old truth that sustains us and allows us to get through situations that we never expected to endure.

We must remember to be "future first" in our thinking. We must not allow familiarity to breed contempt of such a magnificent truth. This life can be brutal and painful yet still filled with hope, even during times of sorrow. This hope cannot be achieved by maintaining a positive mental outlook, but rather it comes by our remembering the fact that there is a new life that awaits us—an eternity where death, sickness, and sorrow are banished forever! We must filter all of life's difficulties through the blessed future that awaits us in Heaven. This is what Paul was telling the church concerning those who had died—sorrow is right and real and has its place in life in a fallen world. But the hope of Heaven is where the mind must begin—to remember that this life is not all there is will be essential to getting to the starting line of Dancing with the Scars.

I have been in the trauma center waiting room and have seen parents as they were notified of the loss of their teenage son. I watched as they literally writhed in pain. I could see the disbelief in their eyes, the instant rejection and denial of the words spoken by the trauma team, because those words were too hard to hear, too unreal, too impossible, too unbelievable to be true for any parents' ears. I have seen grown men buckle at the knees and pass out when the sheet was pulled back to reveal the face of their child or spouse; I have seen mothers become rigid and unresponsive when notified that their child has taken his or her own life. Their own life visibly stops at that moment, and denial begins to rule their thoughts and emotions.

At such times as these, there are no words to offer, there is nothing to share—there is nothing that can afford comfort. The wound is immediate and deep when life happens like this. One life ends and others' lives are altered for the rest of theirs. Things will never be the same, nor should they be, when death or disease has intruded upon youthful vigor and vitality. Sorrow is right; sorrow is real. Hope seems invisible, and, in some ways, even the words "hope" or "joy" seem like unwanted intruders in such moments. Yet, as we all know, the harsh reality is that life goes on despite our pain, and it's in the moments that lie beyond the point of impact when we must begin again to consider the hope of Heaven, the future for all who believe, and the reason that sorrow and hope can be companions when life happens.

I have often considered the cruelty of life when an event takes place that shakes a person to the core—when everything and everybody in life ought to stop and take notice—yet the bills keep coming, the world marches on, the job expects you to return, the school requires your attendance. Life just keeps happening even when we believe that it should stop and pay attention to how a person's heart and life have been intruded upon, leaving scars that seem to last forever.

Recently I was called out as police chaplain on two separate incidents in the same week, both involving deaths, both from natural causes, both a part of the natural order of life. But, this is where the commonality between the events ends. The first call-out was to the home of a man who had gone to bed seemingly fine. When his wife noticed that he hadn't gotten up at his normal time to get ready for work, she checked on him, only to be greeted by the horror that he was dead. In our world today, chaplains are called out only to scenes where they are requested, and when I arrived, the distraught wife, who had been married to the now-deceased man for 28 years, said something that I'll never forget: "We talked about God. He said he didn't believe, but I think he really did. That's why I wanted you here."

This struck me on multiple fronts, not knowing of any religious affiliation of the wife. I wondered if she wanted me to try and pray her husband into Heaven (which I have been asked to do before), something that isn't possible according to Scripture. I wondered what her expectations of me were going to be, as I've had various reactions from family members when arriving at such scenes, from anger or disgust, to being a reminder of the hope of God simply by being there. I asked the grieving widow if I could pray for her and she accepted. I asked if she had a church home or any affiliation, and she said, "No, I just wanted someone who knows God to be here. It just seemed right."

Our prayer time went as would be expected, full of tears and deep sorrow of heart. I was saddened by the scene and offered encouragement from the Word of God, and I saw that those words were received with genuine thanks, but with the same thanks one would offer for the condolences extended by anyone at such a time. I remember thinking, *How sad! The Word of God has such power, such hope.* This poor widow was beginning her journey of sorrowing, but without real hope. Words that were more true than any ever spoken, quoted directly from the book authored by the Spirit of God himself, were warmly received, as one might accept a hot drink or a warm blanket on a chilly day. The words seemed to impact the moment, yet I left with the reality that she received exactly what she had expected from a pastor or a chaplain: kind words that that would warm the heart and soften the moment but would not change her life.

Two days later I was called out again, this time to a local convalescent home. I have to tell you, the drive to a scene such as this is a time of prayer and anxiousness because you never know what you will find when you arrive. As I was buzzed in at the door of the home, I was greeted by the usual faces I see when I arrive at any scene such as this—faces that have written all over them, "I'd hate to have your job." The attendant gave me the room number and pointed in the direction of the room. I followed the wall plaques and arrows that led the way through the maze of hallways. As I began to get close to the number I had been given, I could hear loud talking and laughter, and my first thought was *I guess in a place like this you get so used to death, you forget how badly it hurts for those experiencing such great loss.* In one room there is laughter and joy, and in another deep sorrow and grief, which I expected when I arrived at the room. But as I grew closer to the room, it became apparent that the sounds of laughter and joy were coming from the room number I had been given! As I passed through the doorway, the figure of a deceased 93-year-old woman lying on her bed assured me that this was the right room.

The scene seemed to be a strange juxtaposition— laughter and death in the same room! But as I greeted the family, I noticed that the voices that filled the air with laughter were coming from tear-stained and red-eyed faces. The family told me that this was a specialty care home and that their mom had been there only a few months. None of them lived in the area. They were too far from their home church, so they had readily accepted the offer from the Police Department to send out a chaplain. I was blessed and honored to hear the wonderful and tearful memories about a woman who loved God and would have wanted someone to pray with her kids when she had made her entrance into Heaven. It was a wonderful time, and, though they were complete strangers when I walked in, I left feeling like a part of the family, because I was.

When I shared the Word with the family, I saw that it was not only received warmly but that it also found a home: the words of Scripture weren't received merely as pastoral platitudes but as hope and truth that could be trusted—words that were real, words that came from God.

What struck me the most about these two events was the stark contrast between a person's knowing "of" God and actually knowing God. At the scene two days earlier, the sorrow was deep and dark, and although an acknowledgement of God was made, the comfort that comes from knowing Him was sadly absent in the newly widowed wife. The equally grieved and sorrowful family two days later, however, had no doubts about where "Mom" was. I realized that when life happens, people often desire "someone spiritual" to be present, when the truth is that the Spirit of the living God is available to them all the time. No one has to just pass through life when trials and traumas happen, because God is *there* when life happens!

It is also true that there are events in life besides unexpected death that visit the lives of many Christians and that are vicious and painful as well. Betrayal, marital infidelity, broken relationships, loss of jobs and income; Christians lose their homes, struggle financially, and have personal health crises. How do we get through these times and learn how to Dance with the Scars of life?

You have turned my mourning into joyful dancing.
You have taken away my clothes of mourning and
clothed me with joy, that I might sing praises to
you and not be silent. O LORD my God, I will give
you thanks forever!

— PSALM 30:11-12 (NLT)

Is this something that just happens over time, or are there steps that we can take to get there? The answer is yes! There are steps to take over time, and as you are taking them, it will happen!

It begins with an understanding of this very basic truth: This world is fallen, death is guaranteed for all, sickness is a given, betrayal is bound to happen in one form or another. We will accumulate scars as children of God during our lives, but we must always remember that our journey ends in Heaven. We can spend the balance of our days asking why, or we can accept that "why?" is never going to be answered, and that God can cause us to Dance with the Scars during events when we feel like we can't even breathe, where another step seems an impossibility, where one more incident will surely be the undoing of our sanity. We can learn in time to Dance with the Scars when words like "happiness" and "hope" seem insulting when one even suggests that they still lie in our future.

Once you have accepted the fact that there is a starting line and that sufficient time has passed for you to begin to live life again, here is the crucial first step that will allow you to get back out on the dance floor of life and enter the race again:

Don't blame God. Lean on Him!

There are events in life that are so brutal, so painful, that the words of the closest friend or even spouse seem empty and useless. I recently looked into the eyes of someone who had received devastating news and found myself at a loss for words. All I could says was, "I don't know what to say," and we hugged each other and wept. There are times when life is so painful that even the words you yourself have shared with others seem empty and hollow because the pain is so deep, the sorrow so overwhelming. There are things that happen in life where hope is momentarily crushed, the reason for living destroyed, and our minds cannot understand why this has been allowed by the God who said He loved us and would never leave us nor forsake us. Yet here we are, broken, hurting, suffering!

> When you go through deep waters, I will be with you. When you go through rivers of difficulty, you will not drown. When you walk through the fire of oppression, you will not be burned up; the flames will not consume you. For I am the LORD, your God, the Holy One of Israel, your Savior.
>
> — ISAIAH 43:2-3A (NLT)

Notice that the Lord didn't say, "I am the Lord, your God, so there will be no waters or fiery trials; there will be no flames of oppression or rivers of difficulty." The Lord says (I'm paraphrasing), "When life happens, I am there for you!" I have to say, dear hurting friend, that far too many Christians abandon hope when they need it the most.

Hope, strength, and healing when life happens can come only from God. We have heard the adage: "Time heals all wounds," but I have to say that I have seen little evidence of that apart from God. What I have seen is that when life happens, many become paralyzed by the event and never heal, regardless of how much time has passed. I have seen grown men and women with successful careers and loving families weep at the mention of the divorce of their parents 25 or 30 years ago. I have seen intelligent men and women who have been emotionally crippled when life happens, and I've seen loving, caring people who have abandoned everything and turned to drugs or drink to mask their pain. Much of the time this is because they never take the first step to Dancing with the Scars—leaning on God instead of blaming Him! This is one of the most difficult aspects of life that we have to deal with: when an all-powerful God *could* have intervened but didn't; the divorce *could* have been avoided, the disease healed, the betrayal averted—but it wasn't.

In many such cases, God is blamed and even hated because life happened in a way that a person didn't agree with, death for someone we loved came at a time that was unfair, faithfulness at work was rewarded with a layoff, a faithful spouse was battered by the unfaithfulness of the other. *God, you could have done something!* is what we have all thought during such times. He did do something, dear friend. He tells you that He will go through these times with you. So don't blame Him. Lean on Him! He is there, just as He promised He would be.

I remember conducting the funeral for a father and his young son who lost their lives in tragic accident one holiday weekend. I remember looking out into a room filled with hundreds of friends, co-workers, and bereaved family members as they watched the deceased man's wife and the boy's stepmother as she was wheeled into the room on a gurney, having been delivered by ambulance to the church where the funeral was held. The scene seemed so surreal to me: the matching father-and-son caskets tore at my heart; the grieving widow with a broken back mourning the loss of her husband; a mother, reeling in shock and sorrow at the loss of her son and ex-husband. I remember thinking, *Lord, what can I say? Please give me the right words to say in this overwhelming scene!*

I remember this scene from nearly 20 years ago as if it were yesterday, and what the Lord prompted me to say to the room was this: "I cannot tell you why God allowed this. I can only tell you that He will help you get through this." I must say, I have never felt the atmosphere in a room change so dramatically in the space of a few moments, and I believe the reason was because the big question was taken off the table and deemed unanswerable. This allowed anger to turn to mourning and for deep, soul-shaking sorrow to take over the day, as it should.

When life happens and the recognition that Dancing with the Scars is necessary, it begins by accepting the fact that there may never be answers to the questions we want answered the most. The actual movement toward the finish line begins when we start leaning on God and not blaming Him or demanding Him to tell us things that we will never know this side of Heaven.

The next step that must be taken to begin Dancing with the Scars is more practical than mental and is best introduced through this adage: "Never doubt in the darkness what you trusted in the light." In other words:

> **What you believed when things were good is still true when trials and troubles come.**

God is unchanging, and His character is constant as we go through the ebb and flow of life's pains and problems.

> *I will praise the Lord at all times.*
> *I will constantly speak his praises*

> — PSALM 34:1 (NLT)

This is where the practical side of Dancing with the Scars begins. Praise is as much a decision as it is a natural outflow of the Spirit from within. We understand that God is worthy of praise at all times, and we believe it with every ounce of our being, but we can choose to stop the outflow of praise because of pain, sorrow, or disappointment. One of the many bad pieces of advice that is often given to someone who is in personal agony is, "You need to just thank God for it and press on."

The truth is, the loss of a loved one, the pain of betrayal, the loss of health, or a myriad other trials are not things that we are to be thankful *for*, but they are things that we are to be thankful *through*. God hates death! "Then why doesn't He eliminate it?" you may ask. He did! The second death, which is eternal death, has *no power* over those who trust Christ as Lord and Savior. Therefore, when life is good and when it is not, we can thank Him for our salvation while we mourn or heal; we can thank Him for His faithfulness when we've had lapses of faith. We need to do the practical things that we've always done and that we knew to be right when things were good and the sky was clear and sunny. We can know and believe that we need to be in church and with God's people, hearing from His Word, but we still must decide to do so. The ministries you were involved in before are still your ministries; the practices that are expressions of love and service to God are essential if we are to begin to Dance with the Scars.

We'll talk about the timing of this in our next chapter, but the "future-first" thinking idea that I mentioned earlier is critical in the opening stages of painful life events, and it begins by remembering this one simple truth, as soon as you are able to think again:

> *He will wipe every tear from their eyes, and there will be no more death or sorrow or crying or pain. All these things are gone forever."*
>
> — REVELATION 21:4 (NLT)

"He will" means that at some point in the future this will come to pass, but for now, tears, death, sorrow, and crying come when life happens. It's as natural to ask "Why?" as it is to sorrow and weep when life happens in tragic or traumatic ways. It's understandable that we wonder about the unanswerable, but we can't live there for the rest of our lives. We *must* move from the "Why did this happen?" to the "How am I going to get through?" phase. You must come to the place where you say, "I am ready to move forward, even with unanswered questions. I am ready to lean on God and not blame Him. I am going to praise Him not because my life is good but because He is God and worthy of praise at all times, even during the worst of times."

One final word before we move on. I am not at all suggesting that we treat tragedy flippantly or that because you know God, life's traumas and trials should hurt less. What I am saying is don't abandon your best hope of Dancing with the Scars when life happens—and that hope is God. He will get you through. He will help you and will mend your broken heart and restore your hope and joy. He won't force it on you, however. You must decide, in time, to let Him turn your mourning into dancing.

2

~

Wounds and Scars

It's always been a mystery to me that the expectations imposed by some people onto the lives of those who have been impacted by tragedy or trauma are often more clinical than caring. There appears to be a timeline in their minds, and if you're not on "their" schedule you must not be handling your situation the way that you should. Some seem to imply a just-get-over-it-and-move-on expectation once you reach the starting line, and others demand that you "forgive and forget" after a reasonable amount of time. Learning to Dance with the Scars is no easy task, and it isn't a one-size-fits-all kind of thing. Each person deals with grief or trauma differently even though many of the experiences may be the same. I've seen a woman whose husband had told her that he had been unfaithful handle it with such grace and dignity that it made me wonder if she was in shock or perhaps hadn't comprehended what he'd said. I've witnessed a man who received the same information from his wife and ended up with a restraining order against him because of his reaction. Same wound, different response.

There is, however, one common feature that all who encounter life's trials and traumas share, and that will be our topic in this chapter.

> *My wound is severe, and my grief is great.*
> *My sickness is incurable, but I must bear it.*
>
> — JEREMIAH 10:19 (NLT)

Jeremiah, known as the weeping prophet, never minimized his experience by applying spiritual platitudes. He identified what he was going through as what it was. And it was severe! It caused him grief. It was incurable—but he must bear it. Jeremiah was a good and godly man who suffered greatly simply because he was doing what God had called him to do. He was wrongfully imprisoned at the hands of evil people. He was unfairly treated when he was being faithful to God. Life hurt, the pain was severe, the sickness incurable—yet he must go on. And so must you, as we saw in chapter 1. There we saw some tools that will help us mentally, emotionally, and practically to arrive at the place where we can even think about moving forward in life again and experiencing hope, joy, and peace—and even find ourselves dancing again.

But the big question remains: WHEN? How long does

one mourn? How much time is enough time? Let's take the big question off the table. There isn't enough time, and some things will be mourned for a long time. Some things will continue to hurt for the rest of your life. And that's okay! Some things are just that big. So does that mean, then, that you are destined to be hopeless and unhappy and without peace for the rest of your life? Not at all! But there's something we must recognize in order to begin the often-painful Dance with the Scars.

One of the most important aspects of overcoming tragedy, trauma, or personal betrayal is to understand the distinction between a *wound* and a *scar*. Wounds are created at the moment of "impact," so to speak. When the painful or tragic event takes place, the heart is wounded and feels as though it's been broken into countless pieces. At that moment, you may truly feel incapacitated depending on the severity of the impact. Everything stops, and a personal triage takes place. The mind sometimes begins to protect itself by putting the body into shock. Emotions may try to take over the role of the prefrontal cortex in the brain where decisions are made, so instead of rational thought, feelings of denial, anger, or outrage begin to dominate.

In the case of *physical* trauma, "wound care" is the primary focus in the early stages, and expectations on the human body are limited to the visible and obvious results of the injury.

When the injury is in the realm of the *unseen*, however, and the mind and emotions are affected—when a heart may be broken, even though the person looks "normal" on the outside—this is where the way we deal with our own healing and that of others who are hurting could be handled better. A person whose mind or emotions have been wounded needs the same understanding as one physically wounded during the early stages. To expect someone to begin to function fully within a predetermined time of our own choosing is both insensitive and unfair. Both grief and trauma recovery may share similarities in all types of people: denial, anger, despair, etc., but when the stages of grief occur and begin to transition, how long they go on cannot (and should not) be determined by charts and graphs. Everyone is different, although they may experience the common elements of trauma and tragedy recovery. It's equally important to recognize that progress is essential if one is to begin Dancing with the Scars, and if one stage of the grief process seems to have "taken over" one's mind or emotions, then steps must be taken for the individual to begin moving onto the other phases of grief. (Please note: there is no concrete timeline for this.)

Understanding the physical difference between wounds and scars of the body reminds us that as time passes, a wound no longer demands the same level of attention that it once required, and eventually, a scar begins to form. The scar, in its initial stages of development, will be very tender, and if it's bumped or touched it will cause pain. So, too, is it true of the mental and emotional scars that we encounter in life. A scar may not require the same treatment and attention as a wound, once it begins to form, but it serves as a *reminder* of a past injury, and it may still remain sensitive when "bumped" or "touched."

Oftentimes, just when we feel that we're progressing, someone or something bumps up against the newly formed scar, and it hurts. It's much like when we smash a finger or toe—it seems like everything you do jars the painful area no matter how you try to protect it. Sometimes this happens with words: someone innocently says something that bumps your tender scar; another person may tell a story that's so closely related to your own that it brings up a flood of painful emotions, of which you were just gaining the upper hand and from which you were beginning to think that you might be able to move forward. If we examine the physical wound-scar relationship, we can understand how applicable it is as related to the unseen hurts and pains of life as well. Life's wounds will eventually scar over, but there will always be a reminder of the event in the form of memories and heartache. And just like a scar on your body, although it may fade over time, it will probably never completely disappear.

If a person has experienced tragedy, trauma, abandonment, or betrayal, it's likely that they find themselves in uncharted waters and aren't sure what to expect or do. I can't count the times over the years where someone who has experienced something traumatic has apologized to me because they didn't *know* what to do! The first thing we must understand, whether we ourselves are experiencing the trial, or whether we're helping someone else through theirs, is this:

> There is no "right way" to grieve,
> nor is there a timetable that can be referred to
> that determines what happens when.

The second thing to realize is whether you're dealing with a wound or a scar. The two have completely different approaches.

Rejoice with those who rejoice
and weep with those weep.

— ROMANS 12:15 (NKJV)

Too often, many expect a person to return to "rejoicing" even though they have been wounded when the appropriate thing to do is to weep with them. They are likely thinking, *Am I ever going to get through this?* while those near to them may be wondering the same thing. It's during those times that one often says words that appear to the recipient to be uncaring and hurtful. According to our way of thinking, the wounded ones are expected to have "scarred over" by now and should have returned to full function, when in reality, what is needful is continued wound care, weeping, compassion, and understanding. Again, it's important to note that there are times when it is obvious that someone has failed to move forward in a healthy manner and that appropriate action needs to be taken. They may want to seek help from a Christian mental health professional, or, if anger and doubts about God are preventing the healing, then a pastor should be sought out to give counsel from the Word once it becomes clear that you or someone else is being shaped by the event and failing to develop a scar.

I'm reminded of a couple I knew who had continual problems in their marriage. I was surprised at the immature manner in which the wife approached conflict resolution in their relationship until I found out that she had lost her mother before she was a teenager. In some ways, although she was a successful business professional, she was still 12 years old when it came to facing emotionally difficult circumstances. It became clear that there had been improper "wound care" early in her life that had left her unprepared to deal with difficult situations in life. Her responses to some of the emotional (even though ordinary) circumstances in life were more on the level of a great tragedy and were disproportionate to the situation. Something that had happened years ago was acting as the control mechanism for her emotions. The wound was still open because it hadn't received proper care, and being able to "Dance with the Scars" of her mother's death had never been achieved. Just as wounds eventually become scars when they happen on the body, they also become scars when they happen in the heart and the mind.

This serves to remind us that all major wounds leave scars, and emotional and physical wounds are no exception because they leave behind evidence of the moment of impact or the event. One of the more difficult things to deal with, as a compassionate friend or loved one, is early life traumas. Although you weren't present at the point of impact, you clearly see the aftermath or the scars. Those who may have seen a loved one lying on a hospital bed or who attended the funeral of a friend's spouse or child can more readily understand their grief and the pain. But if you weren't present, or a part of someone's life, when the trauma occurred, you must remember that your not being an eyewitness to the cause of the scar *doesn't lessen the pain of the event in the life of the one who experienced it.* I've had more people than I care to remember come to my office and share stories of hard-hearted statements made by those who expected them to be "better by now" or "over it" or who just didn't want to deal with the person's grief because they hadn't been there and didn't understand. Imagine someone who was injured in a car accident and had a large laceration on his leg. Maybe you didn't know him when it happened, but you heard that it had been a major injury that required many stitches. Just because it happened 20 years ago, would you expect that there wouldn't be a scar if he were to roll up his pant leg for you? Of course not! The same is true for the emotional and mental injuries from early life.

> All major wounds leave scars,
> even in the lives of Christians, including in the
> unseen areas of the mind and heart.

This brings us to an area of life that many of us experience, and that is when the pain inflicted upon you wasn't the devastating "life happens" trauma but the unresolved

pains and sorrows that were forced upon you by someone else's betrayal or sin: the molested child, the betrayed
spouse, the person who has been wronged by another
who remains yet unrepentant and indifferent to the pain
they've caused. It's often true that the loss of a loved one
is easier to recover from than the betrayal of someone
who still lives but is unconcerned about the pain they've
caused you. To hurt over something from the past isn't
a lapse of faith nor does it indicate a lack of trust. Faith
doesn't remove the scar on the leg of the accident victim nor does it remove it from the mind and emotions of
those wounded in life. Yes, God transforms and renews
the mind. Yes, God sets us free indeed. But we would do
well to remember the saying, "The only man-made thing
in Heaven will be the scars on Jesus."

Scars are reminders of the past, and they are part of
God's design of the human body and psyche. I have a
large scar on my knee from an injury that occurred in
third grade that required multiple stitches inside and out.
I was immobilized from it and had to sit in either a chair
or a wheelchair for some time before I was able to put
any weight on it. It was even longer before I could start
to bend my knee without fear of tearing the stitches. Third
grade was a long time ago for me, and yet the scar, though
somewhat faded, is still quite visible when I wear shorts.
The reason I share that is because most people don't
know that I have this scar. I don't think about it at all, and
it hasn't hindered my ability to walk, run, or do anything
else that requires mobility, but, even as I write this, I can

still see the whole scene in my mind. I remember sitting up and looking at the tear in my pants and then looking inside the tear and seeing the huge, gaping wound in my leg! I remember falling backward and just lying there until someone came to help.

The scar is evidence of a much bigger story. This needs to be recognized by those who have someone in their life who has a scar that was acquired earlier in life, perhaps when you weren't present. They may not be comfortable talking about it, and it may have happened decades ago like my knee injury, but it still stirs up negative feelings and heartache.

> Time may allow a wound to form a scar,
> but scars are not necessarily painless.

This is why, when seeking to Dance with the Scars of life, we need to understand that when it comes to trauma that was inflicted at the hands of another, forgiveness doesn't always include forgetting. Can the rape victim ever forget the event? Can the adult ever forget the childhood loss of their parent? They can be healed of the wound, but they will bear the scar. This concept isn't at all in conflict with the Word of God, yet some seem to think that if we still remember what happened to us it means that we haven't forgiven someone or aren't letting God heal us.

And one will say to Him, "What are these wounds between your arms" and He will answer, "Those that which I was wounded in the house of My friends."

— ZECHARIAH 13:6-7 (NKJV)

These Messianic verses remind us of the statement made a moment ago that the wounds inflicted on Jesus left scars behind as evidence of the event, yet we know that He prayed for the forgiveness of those who had inflicted those wounds! Thus, according to Jesus' actions, *it is possible to be wounded or harmed by another and to have completely forgiven them—yet still bear the scars from their actions against you.* It's also possible to be healed in your heart, mind, and spirit and yet still vividly recall the loss or pain encountered early in life. I can't underscore it enough that "remembering" doesn't indicate lack of forgiveness or a lapse of faith! As friends and loved ones of those hurt by others, we must be careful not to demand that they "put the past behind" just because we think they should. They may not have a gaping wound any longer, but the scar remains. Perhaps they have completely forgiven their abuser, but the scar remains. Remembering what happened to you doesn't mean that you haven't allowed God to work in your life. It means that you were deeply hurt and have scars. It must be said at this point:

The devil wants you to spend the rest of your life in wound care, immobilized and unable to function.

Sadly, this is what many do. If you keep picking at a wound, it will remain a wound and never scar over. This is why our first chapter was the first chapter. Life happens. And when it is mean and ugly, some resist moving from "wounded" to "scarred" because they are stuck on one word . . . "why?" Sometimes there are no good, pat answers, although many try to find some:

"Everybody dies."
"It was an accident."
"They're in better place."

These comments are all true, but they aren't explanations. I don't know why God allows what He allows, nor do I understand His method of choosing when to intervene and when not to. But this I do know: godly and faithful people experience tragedies and traumas in life, and many have events in their past that have scarred them deeply, yet they are being used wonderfully by God and for His glory, and for many of them, their scars are now their ministry! Yet even for them, someone may bump up against an old scar, and although it is far less painful than it was in the past, it still hurts—and that's okay! You can forgive things that you may never forget, and if you know a person with a major scar in their life, maybe even in the unseen realm of the mind or emotions, don't treat them as if the scar shouldn't hurt. But don't treat the scar like a wound, either.

Let me add one more thing. Picking at an old scar can open up the wound again, and though we know that scar tissue is tougher than the skin around it, this might not always be true for scars of mind and emotions. It may be, but it isn't always. Be sensitive to those who are scarred, and if you are the wounded soul, recognize the things that hurt you when your scar is bumped up against and prepare yourself for them, being careful not to slip back into long-term wound care, even though a quick outpatient visit might be necessary to deal with the old scars and the wounds they represent.

We must also keep in mind that God is not offended by our "whys." He knows and understands pain, having seen His only Son beaten and murdered for crimes that He didn't commit. He "gets it," friends, and He is there for you as you "pass through the waters." As much as we must be careful about putting a timeframe on moving from wound to scar, we need to be equally careful about never beginning the process! There are things that happen in life for which we will never have the answers. I'm thinking of a young friend with a child and another on the way and the beautiful young wife he left behind when an accident took his life. I don't get that! I am thinking of a 24-year-old man who served our country in the military and was killed at home while on leave. I don't understand that! My dear friend, Pastor Chuck Smith, shared counsel through the years that is a fitting reminder here, and that is:

> Never exchange what you do know,
> for what you don't know.

Life brings things that we don't understand, but during those times, what we do know is that *God is an ever-present help in time of need*. The transition from wound to scar has to have a starting point, and the starting point is different for everyone but we all share one common element at whatever time this transition begins, and that is this: willingness. Until we are willing to accept that most of the "whys" will remain unanswered and choose to move to the "what now?" phase, we will find ourselves mired in the land of the wounded for the rest of our lives. This is *not* God's plan, nor His best, for any of our lives! There are a thousand "whys" that we'll encounter in life, and they will either own us—or we will own them. Failing to move forward until you get answers to the unanswerable can leave you with a life experience that is one continual wound. The sexually abused have a scar that they won't ever lose; the betrayed spouse has a scar that he or she will carry throughout the rest of his or her life. Imagine lying in a hospital bed refusing to leave until God tells you *why* the accident happened! We would never do that, even though we might spend our whole lives wondering why something happened. The same principle must be applied to the emotional and mental (memories) scars of life.

It's true that there is no timeline for healing, but it's also true that if we observe the human body, we see that wounds *do* become scars and that mobility and function can be restored even though the memory remains. The process initially demands great and constant attention, but as the scar begins to form, less "intensive care" is required. When dealing with tragedy and trauma, remember: there is no "official timeline" for experiencing the various stages of grief, but there is a transition that must someday take place for your own mental and spiritual health, and that begins by recognizing the difference between a wound and a scar. When the time comes, be willing to transition by letting go of the "whys" the best that you can and moving on toward the starting line. As your wound becomes a scar, you will begin to learn how to Dance with the Scars!

In our next chapter, we'll begin to look at some specific life events that may not involve death or disease but are no less traumatic to the mind and emotions. People who experience these, too, must learn to Dance with the Scars. Not every chapter will apply to your life experience directly, but every chapter will certainly apply to life around you. Perhaps your role is not one of personal experience, but I can guarantee that you know people who have experienced the subject matter in each chapter, and you can learn how to help someone else to Dance with the Scars, just as you are.

3

~

Friendly Fire

THE WOUNDS OF A FRIEND

The first life event that often causes wounds are the words of another that cut deeply and create pain and sorrow of heart. I have addressed this subject first for the simple reason that it's more common than some of the others. Everyone has experienced a damaged or broken relationship in his or her life. It may have been caused by a friend or family member, a co-worker or neighbor, or almost any relationship in which words are exchanged. The tools that will be introduced in this chapter will also be foundational to the others, as the end result is what is in view in this book. The trauma has already occurred, the relationship has already been broken, the illness has taken its toll, the divorce has been finalized. The goal of this book is to show hurting people how to move forward when the wound has taken place and it's time for the scars to form.

I want you to read this entire chapter through, as there are two very important components to this subject. The first is identified through a saying that many of us may have repeated as kids:

> **"Sticks and stones may break my bones, but names will never hurt me."**

This is one of the earliest deceptions that we have learned to use as a coping mechanism, and it's not only untrue, but it's detrimental to the development of healthy skills in handling conflict. The problem with the childhood adage is that it's a combination of a half-truth and a huge lie. Sticks and stones may break my bones—this is true. Names (words) will never hurt me—this is not only a lie, but it is the polar opposite of what is true. Broken bones heal much more quickly than broken hearts and relationships that have resulted from hurtful words.

> *Faithful are the wounds of a friend,*
> *But the kisses of an enemy are deceitful.*
>
> — PROVERBS 27:6 (NKJV)

We understand the old adage well: "Keep your friends close and your enemies closer," with the point being that you don't need to worry about a friend, but you always need to keep an eye on what your enemy is up to. But what happens when the wounds of a friend are unfaithful—when a trusted person in your life is the one who has thrown the verbal "sticks and stones," and a heart or relationship lies broken and unable to mend? Can this one, too, Dance with the Scars? The answer is a resounding, yes! But it will take both time and practical tactics to do so. We need to pause and recognize a reality before we move ahead, and this is that overcoming and healing a relationship takes both parties' cooperation. I bring this up because as some of you read this chapter and seek to apply the truths of the Word to your situation, the broken relationship may not be repaired due to the other person(s) involved. It's a sad truth that many will make their way through life with unmended relationships—siblings that never speak, friendships that are never restored—yet this is completely avoidable if only both parties would follow God's rules and not their feelings.

If it is possible, as much as depends on you,
live peaceably with all men.

— ROMANS 12:18 (NKJV)

This chapter is written for those who are going along in life, accompanied by a badly damaged or severed relationship, to help you to understand that you must do what God requires so that you can carry on, knowing that you've done all you could. The Bible acknowledges that peace is not always possible between two parties, but even if you're the only one willing to pursue peace, you can at least move forward with the scar of a broken relationship, unburdened of the nagging guilt of not having done what you knew you should. Dancing with the Scars of a severed relationship is impossible when continuing in personal disobedience. For some of you who are hesitating as you read this, let me mention that there are people in life whom we could well describe as "toxic," maybe even just to you. A reminder is in order that this book is for and about you and not for those over whom you have no control and who might be among those toxic people with whom you may never be reconciled. This chapter is not about laying the entire responsibility of restoring severed relationships on you. It's about how to prevent yourself from being ruled by others' emotions and allowing your own wounds to scar over.

When *words that wound* come in the form of friendly fire, meaning from those you shouldn't have to worry about, e.g., family members, close friends, etc., there are several important things to consider. The first is something my wife Teri and I adopted as a practice a long time ago. It's not easy, and it requires some brutal self-examination and honesty, but when wounded by friendly fire, we ask ourselves a question: "Is there any truth in what was said?" Sometimes we miss the truth of a message because of the method of the messenger, or because the words hurt so much coming from that particular source that we simply can't allow ourselves to accept them as truth. We had a toxic person in our life for a few years when we were younger who said things that could best be described as "chocolate daggers." They were offered as well-meaning and loving, but looking back, it's clear that they were mean-spirited and controlling. It was during this season that we adopted this practice of examining everything said to us for any elements of truth that could help us to grow, even if the intent and source were meant for evil and not for good.

There are other times when spoken words wound us even though the intent isn't meant to harm us and the spirit behind them is in our best interest. We must all recognize that sometimes there's just no good or easy way to say a hard thing. The point is that there are differences in word wounds. Some hurt our pride and nothing more; some hurt our souls and are intended to. This distinction has to be made in order to identify the means through which a wound can become a scar. I also don't want to treat lightly this aspect of learning how to Dance with the Scars that have been created by the words of others. Words matter. Consider the reality that people can have their eternal destinies changed by "hearing the Word of God." Words are powerful; words can impact a person's life for the remainder of it, and there are far too many relationships that have been broken because someone was a little too honest or candid with their words, even though they were true.

A fool vents all his feelings,
But a wise man holds them back.

— PROVERBS 29:11 (NKJV)

Hurtful words that severed what was once a wonderful loving friendship, harmed a marriage, or tore apart a family could often have been avoided if they had been chosen more carefully or examined for truth by the recipient. Proverbs also tells us that not everything that we're thinking needs to be said, and that it's foolish sometimes to "vent" to one another and then expect the other person to just overlook the vented words when we offer an apology, or an "I didn't really mean it" was said. In my marriage book, *Happily, Even After*, we made the point in one of the chapters that "Words can create wounds that other words cannot heal." Proverbs 29:11 is important for us all to remember in any relationship where communication is frequent and emotions are involved. This is what is in view in this chapter and not the vitriolic spewing of those who may attack you with words simply because of what you believe or because they have issues with anger or self-control. The verbal abuser can wound the heart just as the physical abuser can hurt the body.

Examining conversations that contained hurtful words, looking for truth from those we trust and love who may cross the line at times, is worth it when the relationship itself is worth preserving, even if it means enduring friendly fire. The second thing to note is that there are times when things come out differently from the way they were intended and somehow got jumbled up between the brain and the tongue. I've had more than one laugh with a well-meaning person as I greet them at the door after church who has said to me after a service; "Wow, you have gotten way better!" I can almost see the scene in their mind playing out almost in slow motion as a pained look comes over their face and they blurt out, "I didn't mean you were lousy before!" I'm always blessed to let them off the hook and tell them that I'm glad that I'm improving as a communicator of the gospel and that it's evident that I'm growing. I could choose to walk away from that comment feeling insulted even though it was heartfelt and truly meant as a compliment.

This can happen to anyone and usually does to everyone. The point is, lifelong relationships have ended or been damaged either because the person hit by friendly fire wasn't willing to examine the incident for any truth that might be taken from it nor to even allow someone a little latitude and accept that maybe what was said was an innocent misstatement that was taken differently from the way it was intended. Too often, instead of immediate resolution, which can come by taking these first two steps in handling friendly fire, resentment begins to fester, and the relationship is damaged—all too often, permanently. Those are two easily resolvable situations if we are only willing to lay aside pride for the sake of the relationship and learn to grow from the faithful "word wounds" of a trusted friend.

But what if the friend keeps firing? What if the friend has the same last name and said, "I do" with you in the past? What then? What if there is no escape, or the person is forced upon you through work, school, or family? What if there's no desire on the other end for reconciling and when hurting you with more words seems to be their goal and pleasure? That is when we need more than a half-true childhood saying to get us through. I've seen the end result of someone who's been beaten down with words far too often. They lack self-assurance; they often end up with a hyper-critical spirit—usually of self, but often of others too; they lack confidence or a sense of personal value. These are the scars from encountering toxic people. Can one dance with these "word-caused" scars again? Can the spouse of a constant critic have joy in his or her life? Can the child of a critical parent find their place in God's plan and enjoy a life of serving Him, or are they destined to become products defined only by the criticisms of others? Although words may not break bones, they do break hearts and relationships. This too can become a scar, a memory, and hope, joy, and peace can be found after encountering the wounds of a friend. Again... how?

> *Finally, brethren, whatever things are true, whatever things are noble, whatever things are just, whatever things are pure, whatever things are lovely, whatever things are of good report, if there is any virtue and if there is anything praiseworthy— meditate on these things.*
>
> *— PHILIPPIANS 4:8 (NKJV)*

The application of this verse as it applies to this chapter is twofold: First, recognize that one of the most important "treatments" for recovering from word wounds is to remember, while accepting any truth a criticism may contain, to also recognize that a critical spirit says more about the critic than the criticized. When this happens, we are to look for the good in others and mediate, focus, on those things. Second, we also know that not everyone who creates word wounds is a Christian, and there is nothing loving and pure to meditate on in the sense of why the word wounds are created. This means that the noble, just, pure, lovely, things of good report, virtue, and praiseworthiness are going to have to be focused on without that person in view. What I mean by this is that you will need some positive distractions when the word wounds become a constant barrage from an uncaring source. It's easy during times like these for the situation to become all-consuming. You find that it becomes your daily meditation, your focus, and this isn't healthy for you, even when you can't do anything about the unhealthy person's presence in your life. This is where a healthy church family comes in, and your participation in those noble, just, pure, lovely things of virtue and good report can be helpful in overcoming friendly fire.

I read a statement the other day that said, "Some people find fault like there is a reward for it." Such people are hard on our joy, especially when they are family members, whether by marriage or by birth, or when they are fellow Christians. (We'll talk more about that in chapter 8.)

It's in situations that are impossible to change that we must remember:

We are not defined by the words of others.

Our worth and value as Christians is in Christ. We are not perfect but are being perfected, and when encountering someone who seems to believe that they have "the ministry of criticism," we need to keep in mind the "noble, just, and pure" things about them as ones who also are in Christ. It's not easy, but it's essential! Just like any pastor, I have my critics and counselors—those who disagree with me, or who tell me that I should have said "this" or "that," or who inform me of what *they* would have said. I must say that it isn't always easy to have these conversations without getting a bit defensive in my mind. I also have to say that in some of these cases, not all, I have come to enjoy the exchanges because I've realized that the intentions of some, not all, *are* noble, pure, and lovely. The person sharing with me is doing so in hopes of helping me or adding to what the Lord has already given me and wanting me to do better, but I had to *look* for this in order to see it. After all, you'll never find what you're not looking for!

When encountering words that wound, we also need to remember that the things Paul wrote about in Philippians are true about us as well, and we're not the sum total of our weaknesses. Everybody has weaknesses, and those who see you as only those weaknesses are the ones with the problem. Your value isn't defined by their words. It's not easy to let "wounding words" go or to act like they don't hurt us, because they do! So when we come under friendly fire, we must heed the counsel of Paul and meditate on praiseworthy things in the ones doing the "firing." Now, I do have to say that as Christians we aren't called to be mindless, spineless door mats that any and everyone may wipe their feet on, but we do have a God-tempered response mechanism in the Holy Spirit and defined by the Word of God. The fact is that doing what pleases God when under friendly fire is personally uplifting. Sometimes Christians find themselves returning friendly fire, which may obviously compound the issue, but the answer isn't to merely "do nothing." The answer is to "do the right thing," the God thing. Keep in mind: the goal of this chapter and this book is not *how to change others* or how to stop the flow of word wounds. The focus of this book is you: how to live *with* the unchangeable or irreconcilable or irreparable when you have done as much as depends on you to be at peace.

Too many Christians allow word wounds to become infected by ignoring biblical instruction, and they wind up bitter and discouraged, giving more power to the words of another than is due. You might be thinking, *This is not easy!* You're right, but it's a lot harder when compounded by personal disobedience, which hinders our ability to walk in the Spirit. I'm not saying that if you're really spiritual, words won't hurt, but I am saying, as one filled with the Holy Spirit, doing the right thing when wronged will do more to help you to maintain joy than any other tactic you may enlist. Our flesh wants to change the other person. Our flesh wants justice and acknowledgement of wrongful and hurtful words said. Our spirit longs for these things, too, but the only person we have control over when encountering friendly fire is ourselves.

> For we all stumble in many things. If anyone does not stumble in word, he is a perfect man, able also to bridle the whole body.
>
> — JAMES 3:2 (NKJV)

Remember, the Greek word translated as "perfect" means "mature" or "complete," and James goes on to say that the tongue, though small in size, can burn down a mighty forest, and thus we have the exhortation that the ability to control the tongue is essential to self-control over your whole being and body. We have all met (and may have been) people who have exercised a "Ready, fire, aim" style of communication. We've all been that person and have said things that were hurtful and harmful, although, at times, were unintentional. Our response to these words when they come our way must never be a retaliatory strike of equal or greater insult or injury. When we begin to master this, hurtful words can no longer own us and rule us, and we will have thus avoided the spread of infection through the rest of our body. Again, not easy, but it is effective. I know this, because I have done it, and the reality was that when I held my tongue while being hit by friendly fire, what I came away with was a sense of accomplishment instead of a sense of failure. My focus was, *I did it!* not, *why didn't I just keep quiet? Why did I have to say that?* My thoughts were deflected from the hurtful words and my mind was focused on the joy of being obedient. You might be thinking this sounds silly, or even pointless, and my answer to that is, "I didn't come up with the plan; I just followed it, and, like all of God's plans, it works!" What makes this a difficult practice is that it's the nature of our flesh to want to hurt those who hurt us. It's a defense mechanism much like we would use to protect ourselves if the attack were physical and not verbal. "Fight" or "flight" are not the only two options when facing friendly fire. There is also "do the right thing," no matter how wrong the other person is, even as our flesh cries for justice, retaliation, and self-defense!

> *He was oppressed and He was afflicted, Yet He opened not His mouth; He was led as a lamb to the slaughter, And as a sheep before its shearers is silent, So He opened not His mouth.*
>
> — ISAIAH 53:7 (NKJV)

Now again, please don't misunderstand—this is not about just rolling with the punches and taking whatever the other person dishes out. This chapter is about when all efforts have been exhausted and the friendly fire keeps coming. We know that "by His stripes we are healed." We know that Jesus was wounded for our transgressions, and His death paid the wages of sin on our behalf. But what else did this accomplish—this silence in the face of great and deep wounds? It teaches us that wounds of all kinds are part of life in a fallen world and that not every aggression against us needs to be retaliated.

> Sometimes saying nothing is the right thing, even when nothing that was said against us was right or even true!

Dear victim of friendly fire, do not let the words of others define you, control you, or dictate your actions! Do not allow them to define your outlook on life, for if you do, you're surrendering control of your thoughts and emotions instead of gaining control over them. Remember, *you are who the Bible says you are in Christ*, and all other opinions are just that—opinions. Don't compound the pain by returning fire, but instead meditate on truth, do what is right before God, and not what defends your dead flesh. And although friendly fire will never be painless, encountering it need not be joyless. God thought you were of such great value that His own Son, who remained silent before His accusers, died on your behalf.

I must pause again and remind you that we aren't talking about the constant berating or the kind of verbal spousal abuse by someone whose only intent is to harm and inflict word wounds that often lead to violence. We are talking about those times where self-control was replaced with self-defense, and the weapon that caused the wound was words resulting in a broken friendship or an estranged family member. We must, however, recognize:

Not all that hurts us is bad for us.

There is truth in some criticism and friendly fire that can be of help to us. Don't let the method of the messenger be the reason you reject the message. This introduces to us the second component of dealing with the wounds of a friend and that is recognizing that not all things that hurt are sins.

> *Moreover if your brother sins against you, go and tell him his fault between you and him alone. If he hears you, you have gained your brother. But if he will not hear, take with you one or two more, that "by the mouth of two or three witnesses every word may be established." And if he refuses to hear them, tell it to the church. But if he refuses even to hear the church, let him be to you like a heathen and a tax collector.*
>
> — MATTHEW 18:15-17 (NKJV)

We'll mention this again in chapter 8, because the truth is that there are commonalities in dealing with wounds, no matter their nature or cause. The ground rules for dealing with sin between believers is clearly what is in view here, in that when someone sins, contrary to what many say today, the individual is to be confronted about the sin, by one person at first, then by two or more spiritually mature believers, and then, if they won't listen, the matter is to be taken to the church leaders. (I don't believe that

me, it's not! My counsel to those who have been wounded in this manner is simple: Stop it! When no biblical sin has been committed, don't become ruled by feeling and emotions. After all, isn't the Christ child the most important child in the Christmas program, and not your child?

We are called to love one another, a command that is directed at our behaviors and not our feelings, and not all personality types within the one body of Christ or extended families are going to mesh. I say this because we need to remember that we can love some people and not like them, and the goal here isn't to learn how to feel warm fuzzies from every person you meet. The point is what do we do when personalities rub and words cause wounds to feelings and emotions? The Bible teaches us that when legitimate sin has been committed, there is provision for how to handle it, and this needs to be followed. When friendly fire comes from the non-sinful category, examine it for truth, learn from your critics, and don't become overly focused on the method of the messenger. When the friendly fire *keeps* coming, with no relief in sight, don't abandon the Bible's instructions to you in such times, compounding the problem with personal guilt. Meditate on praiseworthy things, and remember that you'll never find them unless you look for them. For a long time, we kept a statement from a sermon that I had given years ago fastened to the front of our refrigerator door that read: "Love thinks the best, even when the best might not be true." This is where dealing with friendly fire must begin, by thinking the best. As Paul said in 1 Corinthians 2:13, we have the mind of Christ, and this is where friendly fire must first be engaged. Yes, there will be impossible people, but as much as depends on you, be at peace.

> Yes, there are people who do not now, nor will they ever, want to reconcile with you or stop hurting you, but don't let them own you!

Focus on the praiseworthy things in your life, not just the hurtful things. You and I will have to examine their words for truth in order to determine if there was sin committed against us or if it was the truth that hurt us because the method or the messenger rubbed us the wrong way. The truth is, the vast majority, though certainly not all, of severed relationships between friends and family members were completely avoidable and mostly repairable. Do the right thing, as defined by the Word of God, and do so for your own sake, in hopes of restoration where possible, and learn to Dance with the Scars of friendly fire.

Our subject in this chapter is one that we've all had to deal with at one time or another. Our next may be something that some readers may not have personally experienced but that every reader has been exposed to and seen the impact of. The subject of chapter 4 represents a large portion of our society today and will help you and me to come alongside the many who have been wounded and who bear the scars of divorce.

4

When One Becomes Two

One of the deepest and most damaging wounds of life for many is that of divorce. Few things compare to the pain that divorce brings into one's life because marriage is something that is sacred in a way that stands alone among the ordinances of the Christian faith. Marriage was the first ordinance that God gave to mankind and the only ordinance that took place before the fall of man in the Garden. This means that marriage, as it is defined in Scripture, is perfect. However, it is entered into by two imperfect people, and sadly, too often the beauty of the marriage covenant is devastated by divorce.

For the Lord God of Israel says that He hates divorce, For it covers one's garment with violence,

*Says the Lord of hosts. Therefore take heed to your
spirit, that you do not deal treacherously.*

— MALACHI 2:16 (NKJV)

The Hebrew word for "garment" in this verse can
sometimes mean clothing, but in this context, the word
applies to life. In essence, the Lord is saying through
Malachi that divorce is an act of violence. It specifically
applies to the wife here, for in Jewish culture, a woman
could not initiate divorce. God hates divorce because it
violently rips apart two who have become one. I heard
someone give as an illustration that divorce is like having
glued two napkins together and then when the glue dries
and you pull them apart, each napkin is torn but little bits
of each napkin remains on the other. The Bible says that
the covenant bond of marriage is so strong that only an
act of violence can break it, and, like all acts of violence,
the end result is that someone is left wounded. My hope
is not to deal with the causes of divorce or how to avoid
divorce either initially or in the future, but how to Dance
with the Scars after seeing what God described as "the
Holy institution that He loves" (Malachi 2:11) suffer the
violence of divorce.

First of all, it's important to understand that the word
"divorce" means, in biblical terms, "to break the covenant." This is essential to understand, because far too
many have taken this verse to mean that God hates it
when two people file for divorce, which isn't the meaning
at all. What God hates is the failure of both members in a

marriage to miss out on the benefits and blessings that are possible for anyone who follows His plans for marriage. The covenant being broken is what causes the divorce. The sad reality today is that some will choose not to follow God's plan for marriage, inflicting an act of violence on their spouse, and the end result is like ripping apart two napkins that had once been glued together. Both parties end up losing a little piece of themselves. Having been served divorce papers myself many years ago, and for good reason, I can testify to the pain and sorrow of having not followed God's plan. Had God not intervened, and had I not submitted to Him, I would have lost my marriage for good. I am grateful every day for the forgiveness my wife extended to me and how the Lord brought us back together and then into a relationship with Him. He was working on both of us while I was a prodigal and she was not yet saved. I say these things for any who may be reading who are still married but feel like things can never change and that there is no hope. You couldn't find a marriage that was more "over" than ours, yet here we are, 37 years married and counting, and we have a wonderful thriving relationship that grows better with time. So there is always hope—if both parties are willing to follow God's plan for each of them.

But what if it's only one? What if the hope is gone, and the marriage is over, and all that's left are the wounds of divorce? I was thinking of the story of two female co-workers who were at lunch one day and one said to the other: "I couldn't help but notice that you're wearing your wedding ring on the wrong hand," to which the other replied, "That's because I married the wrong man!" Now, we need to be careful about approaching the issue of divorce from the perspective of irreconcilable differences, because every marriage has those. Not only are two different personalities coming together but so are sexual opposites, one male and one female. Each communicates differently from the other; each is distinct in their tastes and temperaments from the other, and most of these differences don't need to be reconciled, just recognized. But what if the mate that you chose wasn't the wrong person but *has become* the wrong person? What if honoring God's plan wasn't part of *their* plans, and the relationship ended? What if the one allowance for acceptable divorce, even among Christians, has occurred, and a spouse was unfaithful, creating a breach of trust that caused irreparable damage, and no reconciliation was sought. What do you do, now that you have experienced this great act of violence that God hates, and you couldn't do anything to stop it, or perhaps it was done for your own safety? Can you Dance with the Scars of divorce? Yes!

It has been reported that children recover more easily from the death of a parent than from divorce. With that in mind, we would do well to consider that comparison because the same phases of grief are going to be experienced by those upon whom this act of violence has been forced. There are a few things that will help someone to get to that place where they can get back onto the dance floor of life and begin the process of

letting the wound scar over. The first is what we mentioned in chapter 3: "Don't allow the actions or words of
an unfaithful spouse to define your worth." I've been in
the middle of far too many of these scenarios in which
a spouse has shouldered the blame for the infidelity of
their mate. Listen, dear friend, as a husband or wife, and
especially as a Christian, you have every right to *expect*
the faithfulness of your spouse to you as unto the Lord.
There is *no* justification for adultery, violence, or mental or emotional abuse. When these things happen, it is
the absence of self-control in the other person, and they
are out of the will of God...period! Yes, you could have
been a better husband or wife, but that's true every day
in every marriage as long as they both shall live. So don't
allow the words of those who are in rebellion and sin
be the words that define your value before God. God
loves you so much that He put in His book how much
He hates what you're going through. So don't play the
"blame game," especially when the one you're blaming is yourself. No Christian can ever justify cheating on
one's spouse, being physically or emotionally abusive,
or even claiming irreconcilable differences by saying
things like, "I just don't love you anymore." When God
is part of the equation, all things are possible!

> *Love suffers long and is kind; love does not envy;*
> *love does not parade itself, is not puffed up; does*
> *not behave rudely, does not seek its own, is not pro-*
> *voked, thinks no evil; does not rejoice in iniquity,*

but rejoices in the truth; bears all things, believes all things, hopes all things, endures all things. Love never fails.

— 1 CORINTHIANS 13:4-8A (NKJV)

These verses from the famous "Love Chapter" of 1 Corinthians make a great point as Paul strings together fifteen Greek verbs to define what love is, and there isn't one single emotion or feeling listed among them, although emotions and feelings are certainly a wonderful part of being in love. Paul is stating here what love *does*, and when someone says they don't love someone anymore, it means that they have quit doing what love *does*, because this kind of love, according the Word of God, never fails. This is important to understand because it's essential to your moving forward after a divorce and fending off the unending replays in your mind of what you could have done differently to keep your mate from cheating or leaving. You must first come to grips with the fact that love can be expressed in spite of how someone feels, and, again, there is never any justifiable reason for cheating or ending a marriage just because of feelings.

We also need to incorporate what we mentioned in chapter 1 about moving forward even with unanswered questions. The trauma of divorce is not unlike the death of a loved one: time stops, emotions take over, and questions and feelings begin to rule the mind. This is normal and natural, and it also reminds us that a future transitioning from wounded to scarred is required, as life is not going to pause, and the world will move on even though a great trauma has occurred in your life. Make no mistake however, God sees and knows the pain you're going through, and it matters to Him. He knows the pain of divorce, and this is why He described it as an act of violence that tears at one's soul and creates wounds so deep that they scar the victims for life.

For some who have had divorce forced upon them, this act of violence will change everything for them. A double-income household will have created at least one single-income household. Someone may be thrust back into the workforce, and oftentimes a wife who has been a faithful homemaker and mother finds herself looking for a job to make ends meet. A person who has experienced the trauma of a cheating spouse will want to crawl into a proverbial hole and hide from life and the world with a heart so racked with pain and disillusionment that they don't know how they can even go on, let alone have hope, joy, and peace restored to their lives. Divorce isn't something to be treated flippantly or like a societal norm. It hurts people. Divorce often wounds the innocent and unaware. It impacts children, breaks hearts, and damages people and culture.

I want to address a few things here for the ones who have suffered the violence of divorce as a Christian. One thing to remember is that you have an identity in Christ that is separate from marriage and distinct only to you. God has a plan for your individual life regardless of your marital status. Embracing that calling and plan will help to turn the wound of divorce into the scar of divorce, and although there is a season of emotional and mental incapacitation, pain, and sorrow, there is still a purpose for your life in God's economy that you need to pursue and embrace. Remember, every person will give an account someday of what one did with one's life as an individual. What he or she did for God's kingdom and glory, not only as a wife, husband, mom, or dad, but also as a Christian individual. Divorce does so much to wound a person's soul that this part of it becomes easy to forget, and a sense of value can often be denigrated to a sense of personal worthlessness.

There is also another area to be mindful of, and that is a state of continual anger that overshadows the desire to serve God and fulfill your role as an individual in His plan. Much like when a person experiences the trauma of losing a loved one, there are normal and natural reactions to the trauma of divorce. However, if someone fails to progress from the initial stages of grief and to move from denial, anger, depression, guilt, and yearning to the final stage of grief, which is acceptance after some time has passed, then the normal reaction of early grief and trauma has taken over, and progress in transition from wound to scar is halted. As they pertain to divorce, denial and anger are normal initial responses, but you must guard against their becoming dominant lifelong prisons that keep you incapacitated and unable to Dance with the Scars of divorce. Divorce is violent. It hurts like few other things in life and is brutally unfair, often putting the victim of unfaithfulness into the double jeopardy situation of having to not only deal with anger and grief but also to make unwanted adjustments to one's personal life goals and dreams. This can fuel a perpetual state of anger and must be avoided.

Serve the Lord with gladness;
Come before His presence with singing.
Know that the LORD, *He is God;*
It is He who has made us, and not we ourselves;
We are His people and the sheep of His pasture.

— PSALM 100:2-3 (NKJV)

I am all for support groups and the efforts of those who have targeted areas of ministry. I also believe that as a Spirit-filled Christian, there is a connection between serving God and experiencing gladness or joy. The divorce support group has its place in dealing with wound care, but the goal must always be to transition to scarred living, and as a Christian, living includes serving. This isn't to say that doing something for God will keep you pain free, but letting the devil isolate us into a lack of service compounds an already painful situation. Remember, this book is about getting *through* the wounds of life and living a life that allows one to Dance with the accumulated Scars that we all endure. The specific details may be different for each one, but the one common denominator among them all is that God is your help. He has given you, through

His Word, all things pertaining to life and godliness, and those very things are applicable in all circumstances that create wounds in our lives.

We would all readily recognize how good it feels to do something selfless: to meet the need of a desperate person, to feed the homeless, clothe the poor; all of these things "feel good." I was talking with a man in my office who was enduring terrible emotional pain and sorrow due to a family situation, and he had come to me to tell me that he was feeling like he couldn't serve God anymore as his heart was too heavy, too sorrowful. I had the opportunity to remind him that we serve God because *He is worthy*, and while we all need seasons of rest and moments of reflection and even time to heal of physical and emotional suffering, completely ceasing from our service to God is the worst thing for our spiritual health. We could well say that "serving the Lord with gladness" tells us that gladness comes through serving the Lord.

As we have mentioned repeatedly, everyone handles the stages of grief differently, and some move through five stages quickly, others more slowly, some repeat phases they've moved out of, and others move through one phase more quickly than others. There is no right way to "do grief," including the grief of divorce. There are, however, wrong things that can be done when life inflicts its wounds upon us, and the hope of this and every chapter is that we might avoid compounding already painful circumstances that can cause someone to stall out in the grief process and remain wounded, never becoming a functional albeit scarred person. These are the tools that we're discussing in each chapter. They don't always feel good or make sense—and to some, they may even seem foolish or useless. Listen, hurting friend, I haven't sought out the latest and greatest cultural gurus to tell you how to feel better or move forward. We're looking to the Creator of all things through His Word in order to find "present help in the time of need." Self-help gurus are often wrong. God never is. So I will stick to sharing the counsel of God when it comes to all matters that create wounds and scars.

One of the things that the Bible mandates for all Christians is that we do good things on behalf of others, including serving even though one may be suffering and hurting and wounded by divorce. Think about it like this:

> If we don't do the things that can make us feel better, all we're left with are the things that make us feel worse.

Maybe serving in a corporate setting isn't possible right away, e.g., serving at church, etc. Then find some things to do things privately that will help you to move through the initial stages of grief and anger toward acceptance and eventually to Dancing with the Scars. This is really important for those who have had divorce forced upon them for whatever reason, so let me come at this again from another angle. Some who have experienced the violence of divorce are, in a sense, frozen in time. Everything stopped, joy ceased, hope died, and you became one of the walking wounded. Let me remind you again: God desires that you serve Him, and He has works prepared beforehand for you to walk in (Ephesians 2:10). Doing those things will help to heal you. For those who may be thinking, *I just don't feel like it. What do I have to offer? I feel broken myself*—I want to let you in on a little secret, every person that God uses is broken and hurting, and you're in good company. Remember, we serve God because He is worthy—not for *any other reason*. We must also remember that God gains nothing from our service. He needs nothing, learns nothing, and benefits nothing from our serving Him, which can only mean that *serving Him is for our benefit, not His.*

Another issue for those who have had divorce forced upon them is, again, similar to that of a physical injury, as we mentioned in chapter 2, about leaving the wound alone so that it can turn into a scar. I know some of you may be thinking that it isn't that simple: *You keep pointing to God, you keep referring to the Bible—and I read my Bible. I love God! But I am hurting and broken, and I need comfort right now, not instruction.*

I hear you! I get it. But let me say this, my hurting and traumatized friend. I had a hip replacement surgery some years ago due to a congenital condition, and one of the things that surprised me was how quickly they had me walking again. They sawed off the top of my femur, pounded an 8-inch titanium rod down into the bone, lined my hip socket with a ceramic cup, and then two hours after I was out of recovery, they had me stand up and walk! Did I want to? No! Did it hurt? Yes! Was what seemed crazy to me at the time what was best for me? Yes, it was! The sooner you reengage in your calling as a Christian who has suffered the violence of divorce, the sooner you will begin to recover and the wound will begin to scar. Maybe you need to stop attending the support group and start leading it. My heart in these things is that you make it through and not spend years in wound care but move forward in life as one who is scarred but a survivor.

The violence that divorce forces upon one's life becomes significantly greater when children are involved and your ex shows up to the pick up the kids or turns up at the school play with their new "someone" by their side. It tears at the heart, and the moment of impact is emotionally revisited every time you see them. How can you keep from being the permanently wounded and move to the scarring phase of divorce?

> He grants a treasure of common sense to the honest. He is a shield to those who walk with integrity. He guards the paths of the just and protects those who are faithful to him
>
> — PROVERBS 2:7-8 (NLT)

If the truth were told, it's hard to see someone who has hurt you enjoying life, or appearing to do so. Let's be honest here—it just is! When we're wounded so deeply and we see the cause of our wound acting happy and moving forward, indifferent to the pain and problems they've caused, it can be very disheartening! It tears open the wound, time and again, and to hear that the kids "had fun" with someone who has hurt you and has forced upon you life changes that you never wanted can get the best of even the most loving and caring people. Though little can be done to lessen the pain of such things in the initial stages of grief, there's an overriding truth that must be said to those battling the constant tearing at the wound of divorce when seeing their ex with someone else, and that is this:

Be a Spirit-led Christian all the time.

I know that may sound like the "typical" pastoral pat answer, but there is nothing pat about it. It is rock-solid, life-sustaining truth. Maintaining Christian integrity will keep you under the guidance and protection of the Lord's will and remind you that your actions aren't based on those of others, but they are based on the Word of God. Some of you reading this are rejecting what is being said even as you read, but let me remind you again, this is not my opinion. This is the Word of God. *Repay no one evil for evil, Romans 12:17, 1 Peter 3:8.* Whenever you see the one who keeps your wound open, remember that you are a Spirit-led Christian. You don't have to like them, but for your sake, you need to obey God and let vengeance belong to the Lord.

I know this is hard. I see people struggling with the agony of watching their ex-spouse enjoy life while their own is in shambles and turned upside down. God has promised to take care of the faithful, so stay faithful. And whatever you do, including enduring the exchange of the kids or seeing the ex at the school play or sports event, stay biblical, and therefore blessable, and in time, your wound will become a scar.

One of the more difficult areas in the life of the Christian who has been impacted by the violence of divorce is when the influences of your ex and the new spouse (or boyfriend or girlfriend) are in conflict with your faith. This is why you must be Spirit led, maintaining biblical conduct at all times. As a Christian parent, you are needed now more than ever. I can't tell you how many people I have talked to who deal with this, and I've seen the whole spectrum of reactions. I have seen Christian parents arrested and have watched them become cold and calculated in the passion of revenge. What can happen is that the children wind up with two bad examples instead of just one. For those who are thinking, *What am I supposed to do, just roll over and take it?* No, as a parent, you are fully aware of the sacrifices that parenting requires for the safety and wellbeing of your child, and this, for many, becomes one those sacrifices. It's hard, it's unfair, it hurts, and it feels like you're getting the short end of an already bad and hurtful deal. You're not. You're being a good and godly parent whose example will shine brightly in the hearts and minds of their watching children. Some of you moms will fight the "Disneyland dad" syndrome, where everything at Dad's house is more fun. Stay the course, ladies! Train up those children by your example. Some of you single dads are going to be facing the influence of someone in your children's life who is the same moral despot who contributed to the cause of your divorce in the first place. Be the godly dad, and you will be elevated in the eyes of your children above the other man.

Divorce is so painful that God likens it to an act of violence and says that He hates it. But like the pain of losing a loved one to death, the pain subsides with time even though the scar of the event remains forever. Can you ever Dance with the Scars of divorce? Absolutely! Do not let the words of the covenant-breaker define you, and remember: God has always had a plan for your life, whether you were married or not. Serve the Lord with gladness. It will turn the wound of divorce into a scar and even someday allow you to minister to others.

One last thing before we move on, and this will segue into our next chapter: maybe you caused the divorce. Maybe you committed adultery. Maybe you are the wounded, but you are to blame for your own wounds. Remember that this life trauma is forgivable even though your actions have wounded and scarred others, including yourself. You must move forward and serve God as you seek to do damage control for your actions, and you, too, may use this wound as an experience to help others. You'll see why and how in the next chapter.

5

P.O.W.s
Prisoner of Wounds

There are certain areas of life about which we may feel comfortable offering counsel or advice, but which we don't really understand from the perspective of personal experience. There are other areas where we not only can offer counsel from the Word of God but we can also give counsel and comfort from a personal standpoint because we've been there, done that, having walked in the same shoes as they. This chapter is one of those "personal-experience" areas for me regarding self-inflicted wounds and becoming a prisoner of the wounds that you yourself have created. Maybe some who are reading this are still bearing the consequences of forgiven sins in your life. Perhaps the act of infidelity was on your part, and you lost your marriage over a foolish decision. Maybe you lost a job because of addiction, and now, though addiction-free, are still bearing the consequences of your past. Maybe you damaged a friendship beyond repair and now live under the pain of knowing that this may never be restored. Perhaps you feel like a P.O.W.—a prisoner of wounds—wounds that you've created and that you think can never be forgiven, nor can hope ever be restored.

This is an area in which I would not hesitate to consider myself an expert, because it's been the picture of my life for many years. My past is dark and ugly and violent. Although it isn't who I am anymore, it's who I was for many years, and the past often infiltrates the present by way of awful memories of events and actions that I wish with all my heart had never happened. But they did happen. I count myself fortunate to have a marriage that survived, but I know that not all do. I know that some have to endure far more than just awful memories that pop into their minds, but they must also face the daily reality of the results of their actions, leaving them to live with self-inflicted wounds. There is hope for you, too, because God is still in the miracle business, and He is yet the "repairer of the breach" and the restorer of the years "eaten by the consuming locust" of sin (Isaiah 58:12 and Joel 2:25, respectively). But just as I mentioned in the previous chapters, this doesn't happen by osmosis, even though forgiveness is complete and instantaneous once sin has been confessed and repentance has come. Like those who have been wounded by things forced on them, there are steps you can take in learning to Dance with the Scars of even self-inflicted wounds.

As far as the east is from the west,
So far has He removed our
transgressions from us

— PSALM 103:12 (NKJV)

Perhaps you wish that you could put some mental and emotional distance between your self-inflicted wounds and your life today. I can't begin to count the times that I've remembered something I did as a young man that I would give anything to forget. These memories come in like a flood—at times from nowhere. Sometimes at night, I remember them and wish I could erase them. On occasion, when I'm driving alone in the car, thoughts come into my mind, causing me to groan out loud, or even weep. I've had times where I have cried out, "Oh God! Please forgive me!" even though He already has done that and has even brought wonderful healing and restoration into my life. I know that my past is separated from me, as far as east from west, and that God "remembers my sins no more." But *I* still have trouble forgetting them myself.

What do we do then? How do we Dance with the Scars when *we* were the one who created the scars? The first thing to realize is that we often overcomplicate things with "remedies" in hopes of changing our "reality." The problem is that reality doesn't change, and instead we need to recognize this:

The past will always be present in our hearts, but it need not rule the present in our minds.

There is one word that can set us on the path of Dancing with the (self-inflicted) Scars, and that is "believe." *Believe* that what Christ did on the cross has completely covered your sins, even though they may be many, with some of them under the category of the greatest sins in the eyes of the world. The British head of a mental institution is reported to have said, "I could dismiss half my patients tomorrow if they could just be assured of forgiveness."

Maybe this is you. You're having a hard time being convinced of or enjoying your forgiveness because the consequences of your past are staring you in the face every day. I've had to recognize that the past is always going to be present in my mind and in my memories, but *I must choose what to do with it.* It can own me—or I can own it. The way that I can own it is by understanding the reality of what Jesus did for me on the cross. I can know that God's love for me wasn't communicated only by His words, but it was also demonstrated by His actions—His actions on my behalf on a cross, dying a death that I deserved.

In the past, I've often viewed myself as the guy that God was going to have to sneak into Heaven lest others cry foul on my arrival. What I have come to know and believe is that I'm not going to Heaven based on what I've done or haven't done. I've come to know and understand that I'm going to Heaven because of what *Christ* has done for me! Those who might look down on me because of my past have no more right to Heaven than I, for all have sinned and fallen short of the glory of God (Romans 3:23). My self-inflicted wounds, which have long-since scarred over, weren't the things that were keeping me from Heaven. My sins, though many, were not too great for the blood of Christ to cover. What was keeping me from Heaven is the same sin that keeps anyone else from going there, and that is unbelief.

I must insert something here, and this is that true belief is always proven by confession of sin and repentance. I do not accept the "easy believism" that's so often taught today. Yes, "Believe on the Lord Jesus Christ, and you will be saved," but all who truly believe will also confess their sins and repent. When I began to believe that my forgiveness was just as legitimate as anyone else's and that Heaven and hell will both be populated with sinners, I began to understand that

> to doubt my own forgiveness was to diminish the work and blood of Christ on the cross.

I began to understand that if God forgave me, who was I to not walk in and enjoy that forgiveness? Does this mean that I should act as though my past never happened and just forget that it was sin? Not at all!

I know there's a chance that some believers who are reading this have had life-altering consequences because of their forgiven sin—consequences such as prison, divorce, broken family relationships—some very painful results of sins that God has completely forgiven. We must come to realize that although there are great and small sins, *they are all sins.*

> *But let none of you suffer as a murderer, a thief, an evildoer, or as a busybody in other people's matters.*
> — 1 PETER 4:15 (NKJV)

"Murderers, thieves, and evildoers" seems to be an understandable grouping, but why is the busybody thrown in with these other obviously terrible sins? The reason is simple. Sin of any size disqualifies us from Heaven. Murder is a worse sin than gossip, but they're both sins; and the evildoer is worse than the busybody, but both are in sin. All sins require a blood covering, and the blood of Christ *equally covers* all sins. Self-inflicted wounds and all other sins—including yours—are, by one's faith and trust in Christ as Savior and Lord, covered by His blood!

Then why are there still consequences? How can I put the past in the past when I have constant reminders of what I've done or when I experience the pain of my actions each day? How do I Dance with the Scars when I go home to an empty house, or when my kids won't speak to me, or when someone I've hurt won't let me show them that I'm a changed person? We've been dealing with the emotional and spiritual side of being set free from being a P.O.W., but what about the practical side?

As I mentioned, there are awful memories that pop up in my mind at random times. I'm not talking about the things that the devil brings up when I'm working through something that God wants to change in me, or when I'm feeling down or in a dry season. Sometimes the devil throws my past in my face when things are going great! He loves to do this to me when I'm driving to church to preach. This is an important point, for it identifies for us that Satan will use our past and our forgiven sin as a weapon in spiritual warfare. But one thing I can say for sure—the devil has never been able to bring up my past when I was engaged in doing the work of the Lord. Preaching, praying with someone, counseling, witnessing—these are spiritual things into which the past cannot penetrate with its memories or feelings of shame and despair. Simply put:

> When battling the failures of the past, do something
> for God in the immediate present.

Go tell someone about Jesus! Do something for a person in need, and tell them about Jesus while you're doing it. Visit the sick and imprisoned, clothe the poor, do some of the things that God has called all of His children to do that require His divine power.

It may seem as though the answer in each chapter of this book is "Serve God," and that's because, to a degree, it is! How I wish that Christians would understand the power of serving God—how it glorifies Him and blesses you. The devil can't stop, hinder, or impede the will of God. If you have a past that you would give anything to change, as I do, you have two choices: you can spend the rest of your days wishing that it had never happened, or you can live the rest of your days thanking God that you're completely forgiven. One definitely feels better than the other!

> Let your light so shine before men, that they may see your good works and glorify your Father in Heaven.
>
> — MATTHEW 5:16 (NKJV)

Doing "good works for God's glory" is not just obedience; it's also spiritual warfare, and all forms of warfare require weapons. So for any who may be experiencing the pains of the past because of the actions of your flesh, remember:

> For though we walk in the flesh, we do not war according to the flesh. For the weapons of our warfare are not carnal but mighty in God for pulling down strongholds.
>
> — 2 CORINTHIANS 10:3-4 (NKJV)

For some of us, the past is part of present warfare, and it can't be battled with emotions and questions and longings for things to be as they once were. It must be considered spiritual combat, requiring weapons that are not carnal. I personally know more than one mother whose use of drugs caused her to lose her parental rights. I know more than one father who has allowed lust to destroy his marriage and family. I know of those who did things before they were saved for which they still experience the consequences. I know that every one of them who are Christians would do *anything* if they could just change the past. But I also know that those same people can be divided into two groups: those whom the past controls and those who have control in spite of their past. Some of you may need to switch groups. Perhaps you're living in the shadows of a sinful past while God has a glorious, though at times still painful, present for you. I know people who have done terrible things and have paid for it—and are still paying for it—yet they are effective and powerful servants of the Lord. Does the past still hurt? Yes. Are they often reminded of it? Certainly. Though their pasts may be different from one another's, these have all employed the same weapon to stop them from becoming P.O.W.s, and that is that they serve God with all their heart, soul, mind, and strength. And so can you!

God receives glory when good things are done for those in need in the name of His Son. Satan glories in hindering these good works by stifling them before they ever even get started by reminding forgiven sinners of their past. Remember, our forgiven past is not what prevents us from serving God. That only happens because of our sins in the present. I'm not talking about working to keep your salvation, because every Christian still sins after they get saved even though God provides a way of escape for every temptation (1 Corinthians 10:13). No, the issue regarding our current sins is our usability. I bring this up because many times the despair that comes from being a P.O.W. can lead to present sins that may not be a repeat of the past but are still sins that hinder us, such as self-pity that leads to apathy, anger that stems from inactivity, and doubts and fears that may lead one to self-medicate through drugs or alcohol.

The point is, if you have sinned greatly like the prodigal son and have come to the end of yourself, when you finally return to the Father's house with the heart of a servant, God doesn't say, "I'll take you back, but there will be a grace period." Instead, He welcomes you back by His grace...period. The fatted calf is yours...the ring... the robe are yours. In Roman culture, all of these things were symbols of a father publicly adopting his son. When battling life as a P.O.W. you must remember that whatever you can see as true for other people is equally true for you! Or, as the saying goes, "The next time the devil reminds you of your past, remind him of his future!"

Serving God and understanding His forgiveness are wonderful things that help to keep our minds and hearts headed in the right direction. But what about the broken relationships, the estranged family members, the severed relationships with your children, or the fact that no one trusts you because of your past actions? One thing I know for sure is that you must never give up hope! God can work miracles, and what is required of you is to be faithful and selfless. When my wife took me back, it was after eight long months of silence—no communication, not one conversation. I didn't know where she and our daughter were, and she wanted to keep it that way.

Though this was more than thirty-five years ago, I remember the way it felt as though it were yesterday. I recall wondering, *Is this going to be my life? Am I going to be an absentee father, divorced from his wife?* The pain in the pit of my stomach never left, and I couldn't believe what I had become and done. But God was working behind the scenes in secret ways that neither of us could have imagined. A conversation did finally take place, and we did reconcile—but it was those years that followed the eight months of silence that is critical for some of you P.O.W.'s to understand. Although God was moving in our relationship, and it was obvious that He had brought us back together, my wife didn't trust me and had no reason to. Listen closely, those of you who desire to be restored with someone you love whom you have hurt:

> ## The perpetrator does not set the terms for reconciliation.

Trust is essential to any marriage relationship, but I had to earn it. I had to prove myself to my wife, and she had every right to expect it—and even to demand it. This is important to establish, because far too many who want to be reconciled with a loved one (or loved ones), or who want to have the consequences of forgiven sin repealed, often expect an open-arms greeting and then think that life should move forward as if nothing had ever happened. That's not only impossible, it's illogical!

I've often illustrated the point like this: If someone goes to prison for embezzlement, one doesn't have to prove that they've forgiven the person by making him their

accountant. The individual's past actions, although completely forgiven, have naturally caused others to have trust
issues, with good reason. Over the years, I've told countless spouses who had been betrayed by abuse or infidelity
that the one thing to look for in the returning spouse when
considering reconciliation is *unconditional surrender
to the offended party's terms.* When you've inflicted so
much pain on others, as I did, you've completely forfeited
the right to set the terms for reconciliation. You must do
whatever the other person needs. You must jump through
every hoop and go every extra mile that they demand,
without any demands of your own. You may be thinking, *If
they forgive me, don't they have to forget what I've done?*
Remember the wound/scar picture we painted in chapter
2? The same is true of abuse and infidelity, or anything
else that can sever a once-close relationship. The wound
may heal, but the mental evidence of the past will always
remain. They can't forget.

Perhaps you're thinking, *The Lord doesn't remember
our sins, so why should they?* You need to recognize that
the word "remember" is an accounting term. It means that
the Lord doesn't hold our sins against us anymore. The
eternal consequences have been removed from us, as far
as the east from the west. The "temporal," or "in this life"
consequences, however, can remain. If you desire reconciliation and another chance with someone, do whatever
they ask, and don't ask why. (I'm obviously not talking
about illegal or immoral things here.) Do the things that
they require to help their trust to be restored. *You* may

know that you're not who you used to be, but you still have to prove it to them.

Yes, self-inflicted wounds are often more painful than those we received from others because they could have been completely avoided. We had complete control over them, and none of them had to happen. But remember, self-inflicted wounds are not the unpardonable sin.

> For a righteous man may fall seven times
> And rise again,
> But the wicked shall fall by calamity.
>
> — PROVERBS 24:16 (NKJV)

If you've received the righteousness of Christ through salvation, you have the right to rise again. If your "B.C." sins haunt your mind and heart, remember that the blood of Jesus Christ that was shed on the cross for the sins of the world is sufficient to cover yours, too. Should you fall, get up! Rise again, and don't stay down. The devil kicks us when we're down.

How do I get back up, you ask? Go tell someone about Jesus! Attempt to right a wrong that you've done, or repair a broken relationship. It's the one thing that can do more to free the P.O.W. than anything else because it glorifies God and keeps you in His will.

I need to be candid for a moment here for those who may be dealing with the consequences of past addictions. One of the most common features among people who struggle to stay clean or sober is, oddly enough, a sense of entitlement. We skirted the issue a moment ago, but let me deal with it directly for a moment on two fronts: first, to the person who has been a drunk or an addict, and second, to the person who has a former drunk or addict in their life who is now clean or sober.

If you've been an addict or a drunk, and your actions have cost you—that's where your thinking needs to end. *Your actions have cost you.* It wasn't the fault of anybody else. You're not like a cancer victim who is recovering from a disease. Although dependency can certainly be created, all drunks and addicts began their journey with a personal decision that led to the dependency and all of its ramifications. Does God forgive you if you confess and repent? Absolutely! Does He remove all of the life consequences of the sin, even though it's been forgiven? No, and that "no" may include some broken relationships and lack of trust from others. So, my forgiven friend, who now has victory over your addiction, do *not* seek reconciliation, forgiveness, and the restoration of trust from those whom you've hurt as though they *owe* it to you. Earn it. Prove it. Fight for it! And don't ever stop doing so!

For those who may have been hurt by someone else's self-inflicted wounds, whether by their addiction, drunkenness, infidelity, or anything else, remember the words of Paul to the church at Corinth, who had broken fellowship with a young man who had committed grievous sin, had refused to repent, and was cast out of the church family:

> *But if anyone has caused grief, he has not grieved me, but all of you to some extent—not to be too*

severe. This punishment which was inflicted by the majority is sufficient for such a man, so that, on the contrary, you ought rather to forgive and comfort him, lest perhaps such a one be swallowed up with too much sorrow. Therefore I urge you to reaffirm your love to him.

— 2 CORINTHIANS 2:5-8 (NKJV)

Let me summarize the words of Paul here for those whose wounds may be considered collateral damage— reaffirm the repenting Christian, because the consequences of his or her forgiven sin are sufficient punishment for the ones who have truly confessed and returned. This means that we are to treat them as Christians! We are to be concerned lest they be swallowed up with too much sorrow. It doesn't necessarily mean that we must restore the relationship or rekindle the marriage or even extend trust where it hasn't yet been earned. It does mean that we offer them the comfort of forgiveness once true repentance has been shown.

One last note: There are those who seem to think that their "ministry" is to keep reminding us of who we used to be. Most people will be happy for you and will rejoice that you are now "free indeed" or moving out of the P.O.W. mindset. But it seems that there is always someone—a family member or a friend—who "knew us when" and may have a hard time seeing us as "new creations in Christ." They can't seem to view you as one who has died in Christ. This is one of those realities, much like a young girl who finds herself pregnant out of wedlock. God will forgive the sexual sin, but she won't get un-pregnant. The only thing that you can do with those who were directly hurt by your actions in the past, or those who have a hard time believing that this isn't just another "con job" to keep you out of trouble or to gain favor with the family, is to prove them wrong. Love them. Understand that they were hurt by you and that you'll have to wait for their forgiveness until they're ready. It may take time, but it's worth it, and you owe it to them as one who has been completely forgiven of much.

Don't live as a prisoner of self-inflicted wounds. When the devil comes at you with the truth about your past, come back at him by obeying the truth in the present. Or, as James says:

> Therefore submit to God. Resist the devil and he will flee from you.
>
> — JAMES 4:7 (NKJV)

Remember that resistance is active not passive. Resisting the devil is not just hanging on until he goes away. Resistance is taking action that sends him fleeing from you. What does that look like? Submit to God, meaning "do His will" — reach out to others, serve the Lord with gladness, take control of the present by not being ruled by the past. This type of resistance sends the enemy running and frees you from living as a P.O.W. for the rest of your days.

Do something for God's glory, because Satan can do nothing to stop the will of God!

6

Freedom from Forgiveness

This may be a hard chapter for some—and for very good reasons. Yet it may be the most important chapter, because the very people who have a difficult time reading about these sensitive issues are the ones who are dealing with hurts that were intentionally caused by others, e.g., physical, sexual, or emotional abuse that happened at the hands of someone who should have been trustworthy or betrayal or adultery by someone who had vowed to spend a lifetime with you but later broke the vow—and broke your heart as well. For some, it may mean that you must deal with someone who lied about you, hurt your career, broke a relationship, took credit for something you did. The list of things that could make this chapter hard for some goes on and on, but they all share one of two common elements: either the offender has never owned up to what they did, or, if they did own up to it, the damage was already done and appears to be irreversible. If you are one who fits this description (on the receiving end), our chapter is aptly titled: "Freedom from Forgiveness." Make sure you don't bail out! Please read the *whole* chapter, because even though some things may seem hard, they will hopefully lead to your freedom.

It has been said, "Unforgiveness is like drinking poison yourself and hoping that the other person will die." My desire isn't to heap guilt on your head for not forgiving someone who did something to you so heinous or harmful that it changed the course of your life. My goal is exactly the opposite—that you will find the ability to forgive, and in doing that, experience the freedom that comes from forgiving the undeserving. Our chapter heading doesn't mean that you are free *from* forgiving others—it means you can find freedom *through* forgiving others. Now stick with me, you who are struggling already!

The first thing to recognize is that forgiveness doesn't mean we act like nothing ever happened. Forgiveness doesn't even mean wiping away the memories of the painful experience. Forgiveness means *to pardon*. It denies neither the fact that a wrong was committed nor the fact that punishment was in order. It admits both, yet it offers pardon. I know there are some who are reading this book who've been hurt by and suffer from the anguish and aftermath of sexual abuse. I know that some of you have had pains inflicted on you that no one deserves to have happen—physical abuse or violence or parental abandonment. I know that some may harbor resentment toward a parent who didn't defend them or stand up for them, or who even may have sided with the abuser and not with you, the victim. Some of you are reading this and are dealing with the reality that drugs or booze were more important to your parent than you were, and no matter how you begged and pleaded for them to stop, all you got were excuses for how they wanted to stop but couldn't. These are grievous wrongs that must never be minimized!

I also know that there are some reading this who are never going to get what they wanted from their abuser or betrayer—a confession or an apology—and sadly, that leaves the victim of abuse, abandonment, or betrayal on their own to work their way through what could at least have been relieved by either the abuser's exposure or apology. I also know that for you to never get what you want from your abuser doesn't mean that it's unavailable; you just have to get it from another source. This is the topic of this chapter, and again, this chapter is about *you*, helping *you*, healing *you*, giving hope to *you*. Is it possible for you to Dance with the Scars of sexual, physical, or emotional abuse? *Yes!* It might be a slow dance and not a breakdance, but you can still move forward and Dance with the Scars. How?

The first step in Dancing with the Scars of abuse is this:

Accept that what happened can never be made right.

It's natural for us to want justice and some sort of acknowledgement that we've been greatly wronged. It's a sad reality that most of the time the victims of life-altering incidents rarely have their sense of justice satisfied for a number of different reasons. For example, perhaps the abusive person has died. Or, in some cases, normal life circumstances, such as distance or loss of contact, has prevented any interaction. Maybe the abuser was a rapist who was unknown to the victim; or perhaps the continued indifference of your abuser to your pain and suffering is still haunting you. Most often, however, justice is denied because the perpetrator refuses to admit his/her guilt, and then the victim is left to deal with the aftermath without any sense of justice having been satisfied. Unfair? Yes, it is! But it's true.

We could use the "starting line" analogy in every chapter, including—and maybe even especially—this one. When a loved one dies, there is a finality that one eventually becomes accustomed to living with. There are other circumstance-related traumas in life that improve when the circumstances change. A divorcee who finds love and remarries, for example, has put some distance between herself and her painful past; the abandoned child who finds a faithful spouse to enjoy life with may find that the pain of their past has lost some of its sting. The sexually abused, however, do not have the same hope of relief from the pain, at least in that manner, and may require a supernatural work to provide the healing that ordinary practical tools don't offer. This is exactly what forgiveness is, in this sense—it is supernatural, and it is *for your benefit*. What hurt you can't be reconciled or repaired. It happened. It hurt. And it's permanent. I want to also remind you of this: *God can heal any and all symptoms of abuse*—the depression and other repercussions of such trauma—but even still, the memory, the scar, remains.

This is why the acceptance part of the phases of grief is critical and is viewed as the final stage of grief. When the emotional stages of denial, anger, bargaining, and depression have been experienced, and acceptance has arrived, this final stage of grief is actually the starting line for many of those who have experienced sexual or physical abuse. There is no denial; there is no bargaining (which means to mentally negotiate with the situation in your mind trying to come up with a different outcome). The depression is real, as is the anger, and you will have to move to the starting line of acceptance with all these things in tow, recognizing that what happened cannot ever be made right.

This is one of the hardest things for anyone to do, because our hearts and minds demand justice. They need closure. This is why parents continue to hold onto hope about a missing child or a loved one lost at sea or who has been reported as Missing in Action. The mind needs a starting point in order to head toward acceptance or justice. To say that you must move forward to acceptance bringing your anger, depression, denial, and bargaining with you seems unfair, because it is. Acceptance for the abused is much like the situation of the person with a loved one whose death was never proven or confirmed. You will have to move to the starting line of life anyway, accepting that what happened can never be made right and with the realization that justice and closure may never come. But...your pain can be relieved and will lessen over time just like those who experience life traumas that do include closure.

As you accept that what happened may never be made right, you must also...

> ## Recognize that justice will not remove the memories or pain.

This is important, because, in truth, what the victim of abandonment or abuse is looking for is a way to make the memory fade and the pain go away, and they believe that it can happen by satisfying the mind's and heart's need for justice. Although time may lessen the pain, and the memories may not dominate your thought life as much as they had previously, the scar will remain an ever-present reminder for the rest of your life.

But don't despair! There is hope to be found in the midst of such great hurts, but it has to be accessed through the one essential key that will unlock it and free you to dance, even with such great and soul-wounding scars. I'm going to mention something Jesus said, and it's something that although it's often quoted is usually applied out of context. Please keep reading after you read the verse.

For if you forgive men their trespasses, your Heavenly Father will also forgive you. But if you do not forgive men their trespasses, neither will your Father forgive your trespasses.

—MATTHEW 6:14-15 (NKJV)

Where this is so frequently misapplied is in the realm of salvation. This is *not* saying that if you don't forgive everyone, your Heavenly Father won't forgive your sins either, so you can't be saved. We know that it doesn't mean that, because God Himself doesn't forgive everyone—He only forgives the believing and repentant sinner, and God would never ask or expect us to do something that He himself doesn't do.

It's also important to note that if forgiving others is essential to our own eternal forgiveness, then salvation isn't free, and the "work" of forgiveness is required to obtain it, which denies everything else the Bible says about salvation as a gift of God and not of works. (Ephesians 2:8)

So what does this mean? It means several things, the first being that there are two types of forgiveness, judicial forgiveness in the eternal sense and parental, or lateral, forgiveness in the earthly or temporal sense. Christ died for us "while we were yet sinners," Romans 5:8, and our sins were pardoned while we were yet undeserving. This is *judicial* forgiveness, and there is nothing more Christlike than when we forgive unthinkable sins committed against us. Jesus did, and He even prayed for those who nailed Him to the cross for their sins!

It isn't judicial forgiveness that's in view in Matthew 6, however. Jesus had just answered the disciples' inquiry about prayer and had given them a model that included the petition regarding forgiveness for our trespasses as we forgive the trespasses of others. This sets the context for us so that we can see the true meaning of this frequently misappropriated statement.

What Jesus is saying is that we are to be like Him even when it comes to underserved forgiveness. The "this life" relief from the consequences of our own sins, such as guilt and shame and all the associated aspects of sin, can only be experienced to the fullest by our forgiving others. If we aren't willing to forgive the underserving, then we can't experience the freedom that comes from forgiveness. The point is this: Forgiving others is about your joy, your happiness, your peace, even your healing, and not the worthiness or admission of guilt by the one who hurt or harmed you. God says, in essence, "I want you to forgive so that unforgiveness doesn't damage your health and your emotions and leave you living life in a continual wounded state."

The discretion of a man makes him slow to anger,
And his glory is to overlook a transgression.

— PROVERBS 19:11 (NKJV)

The example for us to follow is Jesus, and it is a glorious thing to forgive the undeserving! Yet there is a reality that needs to be remembered here by those who have been hurt deeply by others in life: *You are going to have to do something when you shouldn't be the one who has to do anything.* Those who wronged you should come to you, those who hurt you should beg for forgiveness, those who abused you should take ownership of their actions, and yet, God says to the one who was hurt, harmed, and abused that forgiving *them* is what's best for you! You, the hurt one; you, the harmed one; you, the abused one, are going to have to make the effort when you shouldn't have to make any. For those who are thinking, *But they don't deserve it,* remember, it's not for them. It's for you. For those who are thinking, *They never apologized! They never acknowledged what they did. They hurt me, and I had to deal with all the consequences and they experienced none,"* you are going to have to accept that God is right and do what He says is best for you.

Retaliation won't free you, justice won't heal you, and even the confession of the perpetrator won't remove the scar. The best thing for you is to pardon and move forward with scars and not wounds. Remember, pardon doesn't mean that you act as though it never happened or that there shouldn't be any consequences. Pardon isn't giving up what is rightfully yours. Pardon doesn't mean that you allow injustice to dictate every aspect of your life and rule over you. Pardon lets your wound begin to scar over.

Important —

> Pardon releases all of the consequences into the hand of God. It delivers the rendering of justice to the one who is truly just and who knows and sees all.

Let me also address some fears that may be brewing in the minds of some as they read this. Forgiveness does not mean the restoration of a relationship. It doesn't mean there must be a conversation where forgiveness is expressed. We have all seen victims' families publicly and directly forgive the one who caused the death of their loved one, but that doesn't need to happen unless the Lord lays it on your heart to do. Some people must be forgiven at a distance, because the forgiveness is for your benefit, not theirs. Some people are not safe, and a relationship will never be possible or even necessary for you to forgive them. It isn't *judicial* forgiveness you are offering. Remember, only God can do that.

The forgiveness that is in view here, and the freedom that comes from it, stems out of your own heart. You don't have to feel it; you don't even have to have a sense of urgency about it. You need to forgive because it's what God says is best for you. But again, the great, looming "How?"

Since Jesus' statement in Matthew 6 was framed in the context of prayer, it is through prayer that the process of forgiving the undeserving begins. The prayer might sound like this: "Dear God, I believe that Your will and plan is best in all things, and I want to honor You in every area of my life. Someone has hurt me, harmed me, and abused me, and You have asked me to forgive them for my own sake. My mind and heart say no, they don't deserve it, and my emotions cry out for justice. But as Your Son prayed in the Garden, so, too, do I say to you as the Lord of my life, nevertheless, 'Not my will, but Yours be done.' Help me to pardon the undeserving through a supernatural outpouring of Your Spirit of grace upon me, no matter how I think or feel. May Your will be done in my life, and may I truly forgive even as You have forgiven me."

Now here's the key: your flesh may be saying, *I don't want to forgive them; they don't deserve it,* or your emotions may be feeling *Why am I praying this? I don't really mean it,* but the truth of the matter is, no matter what you may think or feel when you pray that, you have just prayed according to the will of God, and God has promised to give you whatever you ask that is in accordance with His will. This means that God will begin to work in your heart through even mechanical and unfelt words because you are praying in obedience to the revealed Word and will of the Lord.

Remember what Jesus said to all who would follow:

> Then He said to them all, *"If anyone desires to come after Me, let him deny himself, and take up his cross daily, and follow Me.*
>
> — LUKE 9:23 (NKJV)

I know these things are hard to read. I know they seem unfair. I know and have seen the wounds created by sexual, emotional, or physical abuse, and to ask that justice be denied is injustice in and of itself. But that isn't what is being asked of you. What is being asked of you is that when justice is impossible in the realm of man, you are to leave justice in the hands of the Lord and remember that

He is not unjust. I must say again, this book and chapter are about when the injury has occurred and the damage has already been done and it's too late to stop it.

> For those who are currently experiencing abuse, the Lord isn't saying to you, "Just take it and be silent."

We're dealing with wounds that have already occurred and learning how to turn mourning into Dancing with the Scars. Please don't read this chapter thinking that your pain doesn't matter. It does. This chapter and all the others are about not letting your pain dominate your life, not letting grief rule your mind, not living your life as a byproduct of circumstances when there is hope and joy and peace to be found—and even freedom from forgiveness that is yours to embrace.

Pray that God will enable you to forgive the undeserving one who hurt, harmed, or abused you. The second thing for you to do is best illustrated by one of Jesus' Sabbath miracles, an incident that is one of the few that's recorded in all four Gospels. It is about the healing of the lame man. Jesus healed on the Sabbath to show the religious leaders that they'd misinterpreted the meaning of the Sabbath and had burdened the people with things never intended by God. They accused Him of blasphemy because He offered the lame man forgiveness for his sins, and then Jesus proved His deity and His right to forgive sins by healing the man on the spot! Jesus then said something interesting to the man:

> *"I say to you, arise, take up your bed, and go to your house."* Immediately he arose, took up the bed, and went out in the presence of them all, so that all were amazed and glorified God, saying, *"We never saw anything like this!*
>
> — MARK 2:11-12 (NKJV)

I've always found it curious that Jesus told the man to take with him the evidence of his past infirmity, his bed, instead of telling him, "Get up out of that bed and leave it behind!" So for you, just as Jesus said to this man, "Rise from your infirmity, and take your testimony with you!" The infirmity will soon become the scars of life that you will carry with you. Begin moving forward in the same direction that you're praying by following the steps of one who has learned to Dance with the Scars, even though you may not have mastered them yet, and what you will eventually realize is that your *trial* has become your *testimony*. People may not necessarily know or even need to know the details, but the transition from wounded to scarred will be noticed by all.

When your mourning turns into dancing, people will inevitably ask what it was that set you free, or, as the Pharisees would later ask the lame man, "Who told you to take up your bed and walk?" i.e., who healed you? This is how your healing becomes your testimony, and you can simply say those very powerful words that the same forgiveness that you have received, you have extended to another. You don't have to say, "I was abused, and I forgave them." You can let your countenance and freedom from forgiveness do the preaching. And remember, "Who told you to rise up from your circumstances?" is more important to keep in mind than the one who caused your circumstances.

For those of you who have suffered greatly at the hands of an abuser, or for those who were abandoned or perhaps never felt that you mattered enough to your parent(s) for them to stop the drugs or drinking, my heart goes out to you, and I pray that God will comfort and strengthen you! I also want you to remember what we talked about in chapters 1 and 2, that the "why" questions are often unanswerable.

Many become angry at God because He doesn't stop what was happening to them. I remember a time when Teri and I were watching a horrifying scenario unfold on the news that went on for days and weeks. A young boy, who was described by friends and media as a devout Christian, was abducted and later found beheaded by his brutal captors. It rocked us both, and I cannot imagine the pain endured by his parents. The "why" question was big in our minds: it didn't make sense; he was an innocent child, just as some of you were, and someone killed him. And someone killed something inside of many of you. I have to say that as I write this, my eyes are filled with tears, and I so wish that I could write something to heal you, something to lessen your pain, something to answer your "whys." But I must tell you that what I can do is to point you to the One who may not answer your whys but who can comfort and heal you!

As we began this dance lesson, we noted that "Life Happens." It's hard! But God is good. It is unjust, but God is just. Life breaks our hearts, and God is near to the brokenhearted. All I can do is, to the best of my understanding, try to put tools into your minds and hearts to lift you up out of the moment and tell you what I have found to be true. God is good, and He loves you. He could stop everything that hurts and wounds us in the here and now, but He hasn't. Someday, He will!

My heartbroken and wounded friend, there is a freedom that comes from forgiveness, but it's not easy, and it requires spiritual power. You can't do it on your own, but without it you are destined to live as the walking wounded all your life. So do what God says to do, and He'll turn the wound into a scar, and you will begin to experience the freedom from forgiveness that justice and apologies can never bring. For those who wish to just forget it and move on, for those wishing that the pain would just go away, for those wishing that God would wipe away the memories without our having to do anything—it doesn't work that way. I wish that it did, but it just doesn't. Healing is a lot like patience: it is taught and not caught. You have to take the steps in order to experience the blessings that restore peace, joy and happiness. But here's the good news: anyone can! No matter how deep the wound, no matter how painful the past, God can turn the wound into a scar.

I need to offer a bit of a disclaimer here as a point of recognition for some. There are physical things that happen to the brain's pleasure center, the *basal ganglia*, that can hinder a person's ability to experience a sense of pleasure due to physical or emotional trauma during developmental stages in life (remember the business woman who was emotionally only 12 years old?). This is a reality that isn't to be minimized. Life's hurts can cause impairments that lead to clinical depression or mental disorders that require medical attention. It's also important to remember that God is able to heal anyone and everyone, so these dear ones who have been so hurt by evil can also pray and ask the Great Physician for His touch on their hearts and minds. I also need to remind some who may be reading this not to put themselves in this category unnecessarily. Life events can certainly cause physical reactions in the brain that stall out normal processes, but there are a few things to consider before seeking medical help.

Ask yourself a couple of basic questions such as, "Can I experience pleasure or happiness at times? Are there things I can do to make myself feel better?" If the answer to either of these is yes, then it's likely that what you need is freedom from forgiveness and not the aid of a Christian mental health worker. To those who may fit in the category of clinically depressed or mentally wounded, seek the help of a Christian mental health expert to assure yourself of a counselor who understands the unlimited healing power of God and not just the teachings and tactics of secular thinking.

My wife and I were trapped in a constant cycle of things either being great or terrible and nothing in between as we worked our way through the restoration of our broken marriage. It was only when unconditional forgiveness was introduced that we finally began to blossom as a married couple. We call it "the moment," because that is what it was. In a single *moment of time,* when true forgiveness was extended, we instantly found freedom from forgiveness! I say this so that you may understand that I know this power personally. I *know* the freedom that comes from forgiveness!

One last word before we move on. There's an interesting story in Mark 8 where Jesus healed a blind man in a way that was distinct from the other miraculous healings that He had performed. Mark's gospel says that Jesus spit on the ground and rubbed the mud in the man's eyes and then asked the man if he could see. The man replied, "I see men like trees walking." Jesus touched the man again, and he could see clearly. There's an important lesson for us to learn from this. The first thing to understand is that this was a *restorative miracle.* The man's description of "men like trees walking" tells us that the man had once had sight, otherwise how would he have known what a tree looked like? Jesus also did *creative miracles* such as turning water to wine and creating bread and fish to feed thousands. But the point of the restorative miracle of Jesus and His touching the man twice has caused much speculation over the centuries. Some say that Jesus didn't release enough power to heal the man the first time and had to "zap" him again, which would deny Jesus' omniscience and therefore His deity. Some say that Jesus had to "zap" the man twice because the man's blindness was so great that one touch couldn't heal him, which would deny Jesus' omnipotence and, again, His deity.

> The reason that Jesus touched the man twice was simple. It was to teach us that sometimes a restorative miracle is a process, not an instantaneous event.

So if you have asked the Lord to free you from the pain, and it hasn't happened, do what He said to do in the realm of forgiveness and then ask Him again. No matter how hopeless you feel, no matter how many times you've tried before, add to the mix extending unmerited forgiveness and then begin walking in what you're asking for, allowing the process of a restorative miracle to begin in your life! You don't have to live your whole life as a captive of a painful and hurtful past! It may be that extending undeserved forgiveness is the key for you because it lifts the burden of a demand for justice off of your shoulders and puts it onto the Lord.

Again, no one, including God, is asking you to act as if what happened to you never did. God is just offering to turn your wound into a scar and your mourning into dancing.

7

~

3D:
Disappointment,
Discouragement,
and Despair

'll never forget the opening game of baseball season
when I was a high school freshman. I was one of those
kids who grew fast and was always one of the two tall-
est kids in school. This meant that I had long legs and
long arms. (My elementary school nickname was Daddy
Long Legs!) As a pitcher, this was a distinct advantage for
me because, for my age, my fastball was fast, and I had
a wicked curveball, too, which had usually afforded me
a significant number of strikeouts per game. During my
years of pitching in Little League and Junior High, I had

my "off days," when my control wasn't as good as on other days, but to my recollection, in a half-dozen or so years of pitching, no one had ever hit a home run off of me.

In my freshman year, however, when I took to the mound for the opening game, I experienced something I hadn't ever experienced—and to be honest, it shook my confidence for a while. I reached back to throw the opening pitch of opening day (it was a fastball—belt-high and right down the center of the plate, with some "heat" on it). It was the perfect pitch! Perfect for the batter, that is. Yes, it was a fastball, all right, because I had never seen a ball fly over my head, over second base, and then over the centerfielder's head so fast in all my life! Someone had hit a homerun from my pitch!! It rocked me as I realized that the other guys were catching up with me. I wasn't head-and-shoulders taller than most of them anymore.

This wasn't a life-altering event, as we discussed in the previous chapter, but it does introduce our topic: What do we do when life's disappointments lead to discouragement and despair—e.g., when the business plans don't work out, when accomplishments fall short, when dreams aren't realized, and when disappointment causes the wounds of discouragement and despair? Some of life's disappointments aren't as easy to overcome as someone's first homerun off of you, the pitcher. In fact, my disappointment ended when I struck the guy out his next two at-bats. This does make a point, though. That event took place almost 45 years ago, yet I remember the guy's name, his home run, and his next two at-bats. Life's disappointments can travel with us, and if they aren't dealt with, they can be compounded with discouragement and despair.

For example, I can remember a time in my adult life when I lost my love for my job. (This was in my pre-ministry days, when I was a young man.) I hadn't ever experienced anything like this before! I liked working; I liked being outdoors; I liked that I had been advancing in the company—and then, one day, I hit the wall. At the time, I didn't know what had happened, and I certainly didn't know what to do. What I did know is that I hated going to work, and I felt as if things were never going to change. It was one of the most disappointing feelings I'd ever experienced. I found myself discouraged and in despair—despair being the absence of hope.

Maybe this is where some of you are right now. Dreams that you'd long held are unrealized and are now past, and you're marching toward middle age or even retirement, feeling like you're just putting in your time. This can be a traumatic season in life when things aren't going the way that you'd wanted or expected—or even dreamed. Can you also Dance with the Scars? (You know the answer is yes, or I wouldn't have written this chapter!)

There are several keys to this, and although it's little consolation, the first key is this: You're not alone. Everyone has unrealized dreams. If you remember, we noted in chapter 1 that "Life Happens" for us all, and sadly, life in a fallen world includes personal disappointments that may lead us to discouragement and despair. We've all read stories of lottery winners who've experienced what many people only dream of—tremendous instant wealth. Yet the story that follows that incredible event is often one of discouragement and despair. I remember an episode of 60 Minutes in which Tom Brady, quarterback for the New England Patriots, said after his third Super Bowl Championship: "There has to be more than this!" If, just a few months after a third Super Bowl win, the thrill is already passed, that tells us that no one is exempt from disappointment! But again, this is of little comfort to those who are right in the midst of disappointment.

It does make a point, though, and especially for the Christian. If disappointment is a part of life, and Jesus said that in Him our joy can be full (John 15:11), then there must be a way for us to handle disappointments and not let them have the upper hand in our lives.

> *The thief does not come except to steal, and to kill, and to destroy. I have come that they may have life, and that they may have it more abundantly.*
>
> —JOHN 10:10 (NKJV)

The word "abundant" means super-abundant, and this is the life that the Lord came to bring us. This is where we introduce our first step to Dancing with the Scars of disappointment.

The first step in dealing with dashed hopes and unrealized dreams is to get new ones.

I am nearing 60 years old, and if I'm still daydreaming about pitching in the World Series in the bottom of the ninth with bases loaded and two outs, as I did when I was a kid, I'm going to live in a constant state of disappointment. If I'm still thinking about making that one-handed catch in the closing seconds of the fourth quarter to win the Super Bowl, then I'm not living in the real world, and I'm setting myself up for *disappointment, discouragement* and *despair*.

The key isn't that we should live a life without hopes and dreams but rather that we should get new ones when it becomes apparent that too much time has passed, or that maybe it's become obvious that your dream isn't ever going to happen. I've had plenty of dreams that never happened, and, looking back, I see that they've changed, time and again! I have hopes and dreams now, and they're both spiritual and practical. I want to please the Lord. I want His will for my life. I want to do great things for *Him*.

The truth is that most of our disappointments have nothing to do with *God's* plans for our lives and everything to do with our own plans for our lives. Don't misunderstand me—there's nothing wrong with planning and dreaming. But as a child of God, we need to remember that He has plans for us, too, and it's pretty likely that for most of us, a World Series or Super Bowl win is not part of them.

But . . . His plans are even better than those things!

His plans won't leave us asking, "Is this all there is?"

One of the favorite Bible verses for many is Jeremiah 29:11. You hear it shared by lots of people as their "life verse." You see it on placards and calendars; it's posted on Facebook and Instagram and other social media. But the truth is, few even realize the context of their "life verse." Jeremiah was speaking on behalf of God to an idolatrous and materialistic people whom God called His "chosen people." In this case, it specifically referred to the Southern Kingdom of Judah. God had told them that He was sending them into captivity for seventy years because they had ignored the Sabbatical year due to their greed. While in captivity, He wanted them to remember this:

> For I know the thoughts that I think toward you, says the Lord, thoughts of peace and not of evil, to give you a future and a hope.
>
> — JEREMIAH 29:11 (NKJV)

Although disobedience to the plan of God may not be the reason for being scarred by disappointment, discouragement, and despair, the general truth remains the same—and that is that *God has a plan for us that is outside of our own*. When the season for your current hopes and dreams has passed, get new ones, spiritual ones, godly ones! Most of our unfulfilled dreams and hopes are like winning three Super Bowls: it would be great for a moment, and then you'd say, "This can't be all there is!" And you'd be right. There is more. God has plans for you that may not involve a vice-presidency, your own company, personal notoriety, or the pro career, but I can assure you, His plan is better than fifteen minutes of fame.

Do you have spiritual goals? Have you identified the plans that He has for you, plans that involve a future hope that never causes a disappointing present? Let me pause for a moment and say that if you were hoping that I was going to tell you how to make your dreams come true—well, I'm not. That is dreaming too small! I hope to point you to dreams that will last into the future—dreams filled with hope and peace. So, dream big, but dream *spiritually* big: dream of leading thousands to Christ, dream of writing a book on finding hope when life hurts. I did—and I *did*.

Dream and aspire to greatness in *God's* economy, and what you will find is limitless opportunity. I can say that with confidence because when God calls, God empowers. You will never find that someday, everyone else is as big as you, and your fastball isn't as overpowering as it used to be, and your day in the spotlight has passed. What you *will* find is what Paul wrote to the church at Philippi:

I can do all things through Christ who strengthens me.

— PHILIPPIANS 4:13 (NKJV)

When we tap in to God's plans, we aren't limited to our natural abilities...

but we have access to unlimited possibilities. And when God's glory is our motivation, then the power to do all through Christ is ours!

My wife and I have taken to recording American Idol and love watching someone rise up from obscurity and be given the opportunity that most will never have. One of the more depressing aspects of the show is watching people who have a dream but no talent. Many take it in stride, but many others grow angry and seem stupefied that they didn't make the cut.

Sometimes, a little honest introspection can go a long way—a reality check, if you will. When our plans, however, are actually *God's* plans, we don't have to worry about making it to the next round. Whatever God has called us to, He will enable us to do! His plans are better and the results more lasting. There's nothing wrong with having personal dreams to excel in—a sport, business, or education—but we have to be real. Don't audition for American Idol if you can't sing! But if you have to try, don't blame God if you fail! Get a new dream—one with His glory in mind—and use the same wisdom.

I saw the same thing in my years of leading worship. People who couldn't sing wanted to be on the worship team. Could God have given them a voice to use for His glory? Of course He could, but in nine years of being part of the worship ministry at a very large church, I never saw it happen, and I haven't seen it happen in the sixteen-plus years at our current church. The point is: don't "Christianize" the same dreams that led to disappointment in your flesh.

Some may be thinking, *I don't want to get a new dream. What if it's just not my time and my dream is going*

to be fulfilled sooner or later? This is a valid question, and
we don't want to be that person who stops digging inches
away from the mother lode. Let me say this: as a Christian,
you don't have to worry about that. Our bigger concern is
remaining *usable*.

> *For the gifts and the calling of God are irrevocable.*
> — ROMANS 11:29 (NKJV)

God doesn't operate like some bosses in the world.
He doesn't make promises that He has no intention of
keeping to get you to do something He wants. When He
calls, it is so that we may *will and…do of His good pleasure* (Philippians 2:13), and He will use you for His glory
in ways you could never imagine. So think big, dream
big! Don't just settle for lesser dreams like winning a
Super Bowl or pitching in the World Series. Those things
are great moments in someone's life, but they're just
moments. You have to live a *lifetime*. Your life is more than
four quarters, or nine innings, or a single game, or great
moment. This means that there will have to be something
more substantial in your life than momentary accolades
from temporary success. (Sorry, ladies, for all the mascu-
line illustrations, but I am a guy.) If God allows you such
a great moment, make sure that you have dreams bigger
than just that one to hang onto when the moment passes.

> Life's disappointments do not have to lead to
> discouragement and despair.

They can lead to new hopes and dreams and can even turn mourning into dancing. One thing I know for sure: no one who arrives in Heaven will wish that they had done more for themselves and less for God, but everyone who arrives in Heaven will feel exactly the opposite. They'll wonder why they dreamed so small—why they set their sights so low. They'll wonder why, even if they did win the big game while here on earth, were they so concerned about whether their name was still on their shirt or the side of the building. They won't be any longer concerned about whether everyone in the world knows their name or if no one does. The fact is that we'll never feel like "There has to be more than this," when our lives are dedicated to fulfilling God's will. Some of the most miserable people I've ever met are those who are the most successful in the world's eyes. They have what many wish they had, but they don't have that which is better than everything that they do have: the hope of Heaven.

Some of our disappointment, discouragement, and despair can come from using the wrong dictionary when it comes to defining success or accomplishment. In an age in which we're constantly being bombarded with what success wears, drives, where it vacations, and we're even blasted with emails about the habits of successful people—whose dictionary are they using when they define success? Are the habits they are touting as success-makers going to bring you real success, or just success according to their dictionary? I love the saying that I read recently: *Some people are so poor, all they have is money.*

*This Book of the Law shall not depart from your
mouth, but you shall meditate in it day and night,
that you may observe to do according to all that
is written in it. For then you will make your way
prosperous, and then you will have good success.*

— JOSHUA 1:8 (NKJV)

According to God's definition, a successful person is
someone who focuses on living according to God's Word
all the time and tries to do the things written in it. A successful man is one who loves his wife as Christ loves the
church if he is married. A successful woman is one who
views virtue as being prosperous. A successful person in
God's economy isn't measured by their checkbook but
by God's book. Much of our disappointment, discouragement, and despairing would be eliminated simply by our
getting a new definition of success and prosperity!

Proverbs 31 says that a virtuous woman is more desir-
able than rubies, and Psalm 37:23 says, "The steps of a
good man are ordered by the Lord, and He delights in his
way." I have often said, "You can't steer a parked car." You
have to be taking steps if they are to be ordered, directed
by the Lord. It is a good thing to have dreams and aspira-
tions. I dare say, it's even a God thing! But I can also say
that even in vocational ministry, there are things that you
hope and wish for that don't happen the way you wish
they would. This is where our understanding and believing that God is proactive when it comes to the plan for our
lives becomes essential to our thinking. I also think that
it's important to remember—and this is a tough one—that:

Your plans are *never* better than God's!

If you are His child, He's going to guide and direct you along the way, and one thing that I've learned over the years as I've pursued God's will for my life is that *He is faithful to put up stops signs and close doors when I get out in front of Him*. When He shuts a door, no one is going to get it open (Revelation 3:8).

God isn't just watching over you, Christian. He is watching out for you, too. He has a vantage point that you don't have. He sees your whole life even when all that you can see is just this moment. He isn't trying to make life miserable for you or as hard on you as possible. He's always doing what's *best* for you, and that includes keeping you from the things that could cause you to stray from Him, including things this world calls "success." I truly believe that:

Someday we are going to thank God for all the closed doors and times He said no to our requests...

...because then we will understand fully that His will was best and right all along, and ours was not only less than the best, but it could have been disastrous! We have all read the stories of lottery winners or sports heroes and movie stars who made it big and now their lives are a catastrophe. They change marriages the way they change clothes. Many of them blow through money so fast that they're broke by the time their career ends. It isn't so with God's plan for you. His plans never turn out that way!

If you're reading this book and are hurting because of disappointment, divorce, betrayal, self-inflicted wounds, or just life in general—and all the things we're talking about seem like a foreign language to you, e.g., maybe you're not sure about all the Scripture references and what they mean or why they're important and even necessary to Dancing with the Scars—there are reasons why you're reading this book, and one of them is that you're looking for help because *life hurts*. You're looking for something that will help you to process things that have taken place in your life and rocked your world.

I'm here to tell you that there is hope in Jesus Christ, and your search for that illusive inner peace and joy can end here. It begins with what we mentioned a moment ago about introspection—taking an honest look at yourself. If you do, you will find that you are indeed a sinner and you therefore need a Savior. You may not be a murderer, but I can say with full confidence that every person reading this book is a liar, some are thieves and gossips, others are sexually immoral, and still others covet what others have. No matter how you look at it or try to minimize it, the Bible is right: *All have sinned and fallen short of the glory of God* (Romans 3:23).

I can assure you that recognizing that you're a sinner is one of the most wonderful things that you can do, because it opens the door for the Savior, Jesus Christ, to wash away your sins with His own blood. You see, the

Bible also says that the wages of sin is death and that God sent His perfect Son into the world to die the death that you and I deserve, and by His death He paid in full the sin debt of the whole world. The sad truth is that many make their way through life without ever experiencing the wonder of being *forgiven* of their sin and realizing the fullness of the Spirit of God dwelling in them.

> **The Christian life isn't problem-free. It isn't pain-free or sorrow-free, but it is *debt-free* as far as sin is concerned,**

and when you're debt-free in the sin category, you are also guilt-free and worry-free and can enjoy life with its ups and downs and twists and turns—not without disappointment—but you will not travel through those things alone. God will be with you. He will sustain you. The Bible describes Him as "a present help in time of need" (Hebrews 4:16). So if you need help, let Him help you! He is the very thing that Super Bowl rings and worldly riches cannot bring, and He is the only One who can bring peace to a constantly searching heart.

If you don't know Christ as Savior and Lord, ask Him right now to forgive your sin, and tell Him that you believe that He is who the Bible says He is and that you are what the Bible says you are. He will forgive your sins and cleanse you from all unrighteousness and remove that empty void of disappointment, discouragement, and despair brought on by life's disappointments and unrealized dreams.

8

Unforeseen Circumstances

Twice in my adult years I've seen our country go through a major recession. I've seen 15-point interest rates on home loans. I've seen times where, if gas was available at all, you were only able to buy it on the odd or even calendar date based on the last number of your license plate. In this last recession, many in our church family lost their homes because they lost their jobs, and anyone who has spent any time in marriage counseling knows that financial stresses put a heavy strain on marriages. Lifestyles are changed, future plans are impacted, kids are pulled out of Christian schools, new worries are created—and rather than trying to figure out what model of a new car to buy, some have been trying to figure out how they can put gas in the one car they have left.

We're all familiar with a concert or sporting event being cancelled due to "Unforeseen Circumstances," but

what about when that event was . . . your life? What if
the doctor's diagnosis suddenly forever alters the way that
you've always lived? What if the economy changes and
so does your standard of living? One thing I've learned
over the years is that there are some things that span the
full spectrum of economic statuses, and I know that a dramatic financial downturn is hard on everyone. Imagine
going from having your name on the side of the building
to having your name on your shirt. Imagine going from
having a respectable, well-paying job with your name on
your shirt to signing your name on the unemployment
application or seeing your name on the eviction notice.

No matter what one's financial status may be, no person is better than any other as an individual; and a reversal
of fortune—no matter what "fortune" may mean to you
and no matter what the cause of the change—is hard for
anyone. For some, the change in lifestyle may have been
created by an unforeseen and prolonged illness or injury.
Add to this the loss of income, the ongoing needs of a
family, and the growing medical costs—and this can lead
to a drastic change in one's outlook on life and may even
wreak havoc on the hope, joy, and peace that one once
had. I believe that most of those who've had a change of
fortune would agree that it doesn't compare to the loss of
a loved one or a serious early-life trauma, but it still hurts
and impacts one's life.

I don't know how many times I've prayed with people that they might find a job in this last recession—nor
do I know what percentage of them also asked that they

wouldn't lose hope as they confessed that they struggle with the idea that God has allowed this, but it was high. These are good, honest petitions and confessions, and they aren't to be dismissed or minimized because they're just as real as other kinds of losses that impact people's lives, causing marriages to dissolve and tearing families apart. I can assure you that, as a parent, worrying about how you're going to keep a roof over your family's head and food in their mouths is no small matter. I can also assure you that your adversary, the devil, seeks to exploit Unforeseen Circumstances and bring about disillusionment and despair.

As with the other chapters, this isn't an effort to instill sound financial practices to stave off such things ever happening. This chapter is about when the house *has been* lost, or the job or health and circumstances and a bright future *have been* overshadowed by Unforeseen Circumstances. Whether these could have been avoided or not isn't the subject of this chapter. Some may have been avoidable and others may not have been, but for our intents and purposes, the cause is irrelevant. Losing everything hurts, whether "everything" means millions or not that much—everything means *everything*. It hurts, it's hard—and there's hope!

I want to share a verse with you, and I want you to stay with me even after you read it, because it's true *no matter what* your "everything" was, whether much or little.

Now godliness with contentment is great gain. For we brought nothing into this world, and it is certain we can carry nothing out. And having food and clothing, with these we shall be content.

— 1 TIMOTHY 6:6-8 (NKJV)

This verse is important because it establishes a target for us, the target being contentment. When once upon a time you were content with the food and clothing that you had, and now everything has changed and even attaining the basics is a struggle, how do you get back to being content? Can it be done? Can you Dance with the Scars of losing everything? Yes! Let's consider a few truths to help our understanding of how to get there.

First of all, I want to say something that you already know and believe—something you, yourself, would say without hesitation when things were going well. You would say it and sincerely mean it, and that is:

Contentment comes from God, not things.

This is an easy truth to quote when things are going well, but this truth isn't lessened or changed by circumstances. Remembering this is critical to our handling of dramatic life-changing events. However, if we think that contentment will come back once we "regain" the things that we've lost, then we have misunderstood the definition of contentment in the first place. Some who are reading this may be thinking, *I know that, but it doesn't make it hurt any less. It's still hard!* And you'd be right. But something that hurts and is hard doesn't change the truth, and the truth is that contentment *can be* had and *should be* sought outside of the re-accumulation of things. You can be content with little in comparison to the much you used to have, and I know that this is true because the Bible says it, and I've seen it with my own eyes.

Let me make a point of recognition here before we go any further: Having a comfortable amount of money to feed your family, to put clothes on their backs, and to have nice things—with money left over—is wonderful. Of course, it's easier to be content when life is like that, but life isn't always like that. Life can be hard. Companies close, illnesses come, and circumstances and standards of living change. I mention that contentment is attainable even when things have changed dramatically because I've seen it. I've had my personal financial situation turned upside down in the past, and I didn't like it one bit! And yes, contentment seemed to become an illusive and moving target. In this most recent recession and the crash of the housing market, I've watched as couples and families have lost everything—including their marriages. I've seen other couples lose just as much financially, but they never lost their contentment, even with one another. Does this mean that they were mindless drones, impervious to care and concern? No, it means that they found their contentment in their godliness, not in their lifestyle. I also want to say that you shouldn't feel guilty about not *liking* this change-of-life circumstance. That isn't what this chapter is about—to make you *love* struggling or *enjoy* straining to make ends meet. That isn't our subject.

As with every truth that we've addressed in our chapters, this concept is easy to understand but difficult to implement. How do you Dance with the Scars of losing everything? How do you go through such a season with hope, joy, and peace intact? Having traveled to third world countries, I can say with full confidence that hope, joy, and peace—and the contentment that comes from them—is entirely possible with very little material means. I've been in the "shacks" of people in Africa who were kind, loving, happy, and contented people. I've also come to realize that the young people who are more media-savvy in these same situations are less happy than the adults who don't know anything other than being poor. Yes, they, as any family, would rather not worry about where the food is going to come from, and yes, of course they would like to improve their living standards. But many of them have contentment even while discontentment seems to fester in those who've seen how the rest of the world lives via the Internet or television.

My point in all of this is not to say, "Some people will be poor and others won't, so just deal with it." What I want to establish is this:

Discontentment is learned behavior.

Think back to when you were a kid. I can remember my dad working three jobs, and I didn't realize until I was an adult that he didn't do that for fun! He did it for his family. That was what it took to make ends meet. I remember as a boy going with him to the gas station or the wood shop, where he worked at side jobs after working a full-time job during the day. I thought it was great! I loved washing car windows or pumping gas for people. (This was back when all gas stations were full service.) For me, it was an adventure. And even though my dad never complained, I know that it was hard. Two people viewing the same situation will see it completely differently, all because of perception. Poor children don't know they're poor until someone tells them they are. We become discontent when Unforeseen Circumstances cause a lifestyle change with which the world tells us we should be discontented.

There is a reality that one must acknowledge regarding losing everything and going through a dramatic lifestyle change, and Job is the man to illustrate it for us:

> Then Job arose, tore his robe, and shaved his head; and he fell to the ground and worshiped. And he said: "Naked I came from my mother's womb, And naked shall I return there. The Lord gave, and the Lord has taken away; Blessed be the name of the Lord." In all this Job did not sin nor charge God with wrong.
>
> — JOB 1:20-22 (NKJV)

This was Job's reaction to losing everything that he had and everyone whom he loved, except for his wife (who was a very poor comforter), all in one day! In all of this, Job did not sin or charge God with wrong. How did he arrive at the place where he could react in such a manner? The answer lies in his perspective on the things that he had: The Lord had given them to him, and the Lord had taken them away, because the earth is the Lord's and all that is in it. This is how someone arrives at a state of contentment—and it's possible for people other than Job to have this!

> *Not that I speak in regard to need, for I have learned in whatever state I am, to be content: I know how to be abased, and I know how to abound. Everywhere and in all things I have learned both to be full and to be hungry, both to abound and to suffer need. I can do all things through Christ who strengthens me.*
>
> — PHILIPPIANS 4:10-13 (NKJV)

Paul's statement brings up an important point. He says that he has "learned" that contentment is possible regardless of financial circumstances, and he tells us that he learned these lessons *experientially*. He has been poor, and he has also had abundance—he has learned to be content in both situations. How he did so, I believe, is in what Job said about everything coming from the Lord. For those who may feel like they've lost everything that they had worked for, let me paraphrase Job's words like this:

Everything we have is actually the Lord's.

For those who want to go down the road of, "I worked hard for what I had," let me ask you, who gave you the strength to work hard and the breath to breathe while doing so? I know that you know the answer, and please remember: this is a tool to try to help you to move forward. In this case, it may feel like a crowbar, but a crowbar is still a tool. When we begin to realize that we've allowed our identity to be in the things that we accumulate or accomplish and not in Christ and godliness, then as things come and go, which they do for us all, learning contentment through *unlearning* discontentment is essential!

> *Beware that you do not forget the LORD your God by not keeping His commandments, His judgments, and His statutes which I command you today, lest—when you have eaten and are full, and have built beautiful houses and dwell in them; and when your herds and your flocks multiply, and your silver and your gold are multiplied, and all that you have is multiplied; when your heart is lifted up, and you forget the LORD your God who brought you out of the land of Egypt, from the house of bondage; who led you through that great and terrible wilderness, in which were fiery serpents and scorpions and thirsty land where there was no water; who brought water for you out of the flinty rock; who fed you in the wilderness with manna, which your fathers did not know, that He might humble you and that He might test you, to do you good in the end — then you say in your heart, "My power and the might of my hand have gained me this wealth."*

And you shall remember the LORD your God, for
it is He who gives you power to get wealth, that
He may establish His covenant which He swore to
your fathers, as it is this day.

— DEUTERONOMY 8:11-18 (NKJV)

Applying this strictly to Israel would be in error, for there are many commands that God gave to Israel that still apply to us today. I can think of ten of them right off the top of my head. Not everything that is written to Israel can be applied to us, but when the nature and character of God, or just general life principles, are in view, then we must recognize that what was written to Israel applies to mankind in general. There is only one God. Images are not to be made of Him nor is His name to be taken in vain. Everyone should honor his father and mother, and no one should murder, no one should commit adultery, no one should steal, bear false witness, or covet. All of these commandments were given to Israel, yet they are the very laws that identify all people as sinners, for all have sinned—and the standard of measure is the law of God, given to the Jews. Therefore, the power to gain wealth comes from God for all people, and the right to give and to take away is exclusively His. When He gives, we can be content, and when He takes away, we can be content. This isn't easy, but it's helpful to remember that it is *all His* and anything that you had was on loan from Him.

Allow me to illustrate this point, because I realize that I'm trying to take you somewhere that your mind doesn't want to go and that your flesh is going to resist. Think about it like this: If you were going out of town, and when you arrived at your destination, you rented a car—would you expect to keep the car after your trip was over? Of course not! And this feeble effort that it took to move your thinking in the right direction makes the point of under-standing *ownership*. If you recognize that all that we have is from God and belongs to God, then turning it back over to Him may not be easy, but at least it's understandable.

We all know that the Lord's ways are not ours, and His decision-making processes and determinations are beyond our knowledge and comprehension. In previous chapters we have well established that sometimes mov-ing ahead without answers is going to be necessary to Dancing with the Scars, no matter what caused them. If God allows you to lose your home while another is per-mitted to keep theirs, if He has allowed you to lose your job and another kept theirs, as hard as that is—and it is very hard—we must come to the place where we can say: "The Lord gives and the Lord takes away; blessed be the name of the Lord."

I must add this before we go any further: Getting you to the place where you can say that may be the lesson during the trial in the first place. That thing about "You shall have no other gods before me"? He meant that! I say this because I don't want you to have in your mind that God's decisions are arbitrary. God isn't sitting in Heaven thinking: *I wonder what Bob and Nancy would do if I took all their stuff?* God doesn't operate capriciously; all of His actions are calculated and purposeful, even the ones that are hard for us. I can't think of a better way to come to grips with the loss of material things and to move forward in your thinking than to recognize that God is good, and if He allowed it, there is a purpose.

We all understand the ebb and flow and the cyclical nature of the economy and that some seasons of life are better than others. Keeping a loose grip on material things, however they come—be it much or little—will keep us from learning discontentment should the Lord allow a season of economic downturn for you and your family.

As with all of our subjects, the starting line begins with our thinking—and it's therefore essential to establish a proper mindset toward shifts in our economic status. With the right mindset, the practical steps now come into play. Having unlearned discontentment and relearned contentment, how do you move forward into—and hopefully through—this season of change?

> For here we have no continuing city, but we seek the one to come. Therefore by Him let us continually offer the sacrifice of praise to God, that is, the fruit of our lips, giving thanks to His name. But do not forget to do good and to share, for with such sacrifices God is well pleased.
> — HEBREWS 13:14-16 (NKJV)

One of the things we all become vulnerable to when negative lifestyle changes happen is becoming consumed by the change and trying to figure out what we can do to change things back. But having it fixed in our minds that what we had and when it may return is in the Lord's hands, we need to be careful about being fixated on the cause or the cure to the point of ignoring normal Christian thinking and practices. Most of us have heard of the widow in Mark 12 who gave her two copper coins, equaling less than a half-penny together, to the temple treasury. Jesus commended this woman's gift above those who gave out of their abundance. He said to His watching disciples, "This woman put in more than all the others, for they gave little out of their plenty, and she gave all she had." (Don't worry—I'm not going to talk about tithing.) The story makes a point though:

> Don't allow a financial downturn
> to turn into a spiritual one.

Keep doing the things you are supposed to do as a Christian. Keep praising God and giving thanks; keep doing good things and being generous, even though that has a new scale by which it is measured for you. There's a man in our church who went through as bad a situation as I've ever seen when it comes to finding work. For more than three years he searched for a job, during which time his wife was ill and his daughter was diagnosed with cancer. Yet I would see him each week, and when I asked him how he was doing, what he said was so obviously real and from his heart that it always encouraged me. He didn't repeat the same thing every week, but he always said something positive about the goodness of God and His faithfulness. He was always serving, and he and his wife attended our prayer nights. When needs arose, they would usually encourage and share with others, even while in great need themselves. It was beautiful to see and hear. There was a second blessing in this as well, because many in our fellowship who became aware of their situation practiced doing good and sharing with them, and thus the body, the church, was edified!

This brings up a point that needs to be said in our day, when many are teaching that "faith can bring a financial windfall." This is not only false—it's dangerous, and it can lead to a crisis in faith when things get tough. It's true that God does bless His people materially, but that is based on *His* will, not on our faith. Yes, He does bless our efforts, and the law of sowing and reaping applies even in the realm of hard work and rewards.

However, if we view material things as the primary means of God's blessing us, then when an economic downturn takes place and unforeseen circumstances occur that change your financial status, we're left with this errant conclusion: If faith brought you financial blessing, then a lapse of faith must have brought this downturn. This is a grievous error, as there are many cases in which people have had their faith *increased* by times of trial and financial struggle, and a "lapse of faith" would certainly not describe their spiritual condition. I say this because financial downturns that cause spiritual ones result in a two-pronged concern. There is a danger of one's becoming consumed by the "why" of the situation and doubting or questioning the goodness of God; or perhaps the spiritual downturn comes because of what someone heard or believed about financial "blessings" that isn't true. I've told the church on many occasions that faith is not the ability to actualize your own "lifestyle of the rich and famous." Faith means *trusting in proven truth*—taking the Word of God as absolute truth and applying it to everyday living.

This would include trusting through trials, i.e., being faithful through trials and not seeing the trial as indicating a lapse of faith or divine discipline, and certainly not thinking that God has forgotten or forsaken you just because the bank account looks different than it used to.

> *In this you greatly rejoice, though now for a little while, if need be, you have been grieved by various trials, that the genuineness of your faith, being much more precious than gold that perishes, though it is tested by fire, may be found to praise, honor, and glory at the revelation of Jesus Christ, whom having not seen you love. Though now you do not see Him, yet believing, you rejoice with joy inexpressible and full of glory, receiving the end of your faith —the salvation of your souls.*
>
> — 1 PETER 1:6-9 (NKJV)

Let me close out this chapter with a couple of summary conclusions. It is our nature to want recognition and acknowledgement for personal effort and achievements, and we also enjoy the rewards. This is, in and of itself, not bad *per se*, but it can be a problem. How disappointing it would be if we never saw any fruit from our labors. It's also true that God is trying to create something in us as we make our way through life, and often, trials are the way that He does it! This is what Peter is saying: *genuine faith is more precious than material things.*

Peter also gives us a great tool to implement when trials are being used to refine our faith, including financial trials. It is that we are reminded of our "Future First" thinking, as Peter points to the end of our faith: the salvation of our souls.

We've come to the final reminder in this chapter about unforeseen circumstances that cause life and lifestyle changes, and that is:

You can never lose what matters most.

The Bible assures us that *nothing* can separate us from God's love, and no one can snatch us from His hand (Romans 8:38-39 and John 10:28-29, respectively). Your future home is Heaven, a city whose Builder and Maker is God. It's a city where the things that we fret over losing in life are as common as dirt. Gold is used to pave the streets! Pearls are so big that they can be used as a city gate; precious stones are so abundant and common that they are used as the foundation for the city itself! Between here and our arrival there, we will encounter trials, and those trials can even include financial ones. But this, and every other form of trial, is not without purpose: trials "test by fire," meaning that they refine our faith, and refined faith— unwavering faith—gives praise, honor, and glory to Jesus Christ. How so? By our continuing to do good, sharing with others, and not allowing a financial crisis to create a spiritual one. The enemy will try to exploit such times and may even try to convince us, as Job's wife encouraged him, to "curse God and die."

What you're going through is hard, and it hurts. But it's a wound that can become a scar—a testimony—if you will view it properly by remembering this: The power to gain wealth is from God, and all that you've had was really His. The most important thing that you have can *never* be lost, and you still have that—the end of your faith, the salvation of your soul!

9

Fractured Fellowship

This may seem like an odd chapter to include in a book that discusses major traumatic events like death, disease, and other painful life occurrences. The truth is that anything that alters the course of one's life is worthy of mention, and although some things may be of a different nature, they still cause wounds that need attention. Actually, the subject of this chapter impacts more people than you might imagine.

Each of the previous chapters addressed difficult and heartbreaking issues that many encounter in life: some of them are avoidable; others are not. Life brings things our way over which we have no control at times, and that often includes the painful actions of others and the impact of those actions on us. Although it's true that divorce, friendly fire, and broken relationships are completely avoidable, it's also true that avoiding them only works when all parties are committed to the plan. In this chapter, we will address an issue that has always been present but, much like divorce, has advanced by leaps and bounds in recent years. When I was growing up, I didn't know anyone who was from a broken home. None of my friends' parents were divorced, and I didn't know anyone who lived in a single-parent home.

Well, times have changed. They have also changed concerning our subject of "Fractured Fellowship," or the broken relationships between a person and the church or pastor. The number of books written on this subject is staggering, which, in and of itself, reveals the magnitude of an issue that again, though always present, has reached unprecedented heights. It's also true that what we discovered in the chapter of Friendly Fire is often the cause of Fractured Fellowship—and that is *miscommunication.*

One of the sad realities of our day is that, oftentimes, when a dispute arises, people start talking *about* each other instead of *to* each other. This is frequently the case when it comes to church misunderstandings or disputes. With that in mind, let me say this before we start digging into the details: If you have a Fractured Fellowship scenario in your life where there is unresolved conflict between yourself and another church member, leader, or pastor—have you talked to them? I recall a young couple with whom I had invested a great deal of time, had seen them through all of their premarital counseling, had performed their wedding, had helped them through some early-marriage hurdles as they began their journey together, when suddenly, they quit showing up for church.

After a couple of weeks, I decided to check in on them because I was concerned that something had happened to one of them. What I heard on the other end of the phone took me completely by surprise. When I asked the young man how they were doing, he replied very curtly, "We've left the church and are going somewhere else."

More than a little taken aback, I asked him why, to which he replied, "You walked right by us two weeks in a row and didn't say hi, so we figured, *Who needs ya!* We've moved on."

I tried to explain that I didn't remember when this might have happened and that if I had walked by without speaking, it wasn't intentional. But the issue was settled in their minds, and nothing was going to change it. I will say at this point that it's entirely possible that this did occur, and anyone who has played sports will understand it, but when I'm about to get up and teach, I put on the "game face." I'm very focused, and as I walk from my office to the sanctuary on Sundays and Wednesdays, it is always quite possible for me not to "see" people who might be standing right there!

Many of the Fractured Fellowship issues fall under this kind of scenario, but not all of them do. There are times when hurts are not imagined but real—where a wrong has been committed and a relationship damaged, including the relationship between a pastor or church leader and a member of the church.

One more thing before we jump in: doctrinal differences on matters of interpretation of last-days things, or whether one is saved while living under free will, or if all the saved are drawn in by God, are points to recognize—not reasons to divide or Fracture Fellowship. I will stand my ground on my doctrinal understanding and not budge, but I will *not* say that if someone has a different last-days scenario from mine or sees the progression of how one gets saved in a different light, then they're in sin and unsaved. Obviously, there's a line that's not to be crossed, to be sure, but I hope that you understand my point.

People in the church throw stones at each other over the silliest things. I was once visiting a church where a famous pastor had preached a century ago and was told by the current pastor, as we walked through the sanctuary and noticed some construction going on, that the church had been debating for seventeen years whether or not to repurpose some of the old wooden pews to build a mothers' room that would match the rest of the 200-year old sanctuary. It took seventeen years to debate an issue that should have taken seventeen minutes at the most! The point is this: Make sure that all that should be done to resolve differences is done before severing a church relationship over non-sinful issues.

But what about when it comes to legitimate hurts and not doctrinal differences or matters of opinion? What about when someone has been wronged, and sin has been committed, and it's not just a matter of hurt feelings or misunderstanding? What then? Can one Dance with the Scars of Fractured Fellowship and enjoy a thriving and safe relationship with a pastor or church again? I hope you already know the answer. Yes! This issue has many tentacles, though, so let me address them one at a time, beginning with the pastor.

Pastors do hurt people at times, sometimes unknowingly and other times uncaringly—and sadly, sometimes, even on purpose. One of the most common and disheartening aspects of the days in which we live is to hear how people walked away from a church because of the actions of a church leader who wounded them, leaving them disenfranchised to the point of their having a crisis of faith. I want to say two things to those who have been hurt by the sinful actions of a pastor or a church leader, and the first is this:

Don't blame *God* for what people have done.

That "free will" thing that we talk about in church isn't strictly a matter of how one comes to faith, but the truth is that God does not force people to obey Him, and people in ministry or leadership positions can "flesh out" (i.e., react in the flesh) just like anyone else. The pastor and church leaders are all fallible human beings. They make mistakes, still battle their flesh, and are as human as anyone else. I say this not in their defense or as a cop-out, but in the hope of reminding those who've been hurt by a church leader to remember that they weren't hurt by *God*, and there's no reason to walk away from *Him* because of what a fallible human did! One of the most important lessons that we can take away from the Bible is that God's chosen people do stupid, selfish, mean-spirited, prideful, self-promoting, and even lustful things at times—and God is responsible for *none* of them!

I've often heard people say: "I don't go to church anymore because of what so-and-so did, or the way this leader treated me, or what I heard that church leader did or said, and I don't want anything to do with a place where there are people like that!"

First of all, consider that statement: to say that you left the church because someone hurt you leaves you in fellowship only with the world where people are *more* ruthless and self-promoting than the majority of people in the church! This is to jump from the proverbial frying pan right into the fire.

Secondly, for those who say, "I don't go to church anymore because I was hurt by a pastor or leader, but I'm not having a crisis of faith," let me ask you: Can you say that you're still on the football team if you never go to practice or play in the games? Although it's true that you can love football and not play, or maybe you can't attend the games in person, so you watch them on TV, and thus you can do the same with church—yes, you can love the Lord and watch church on TV or online, but let me remind you of this: church isn't *for* you; "you" are *for* the church! Because you are on the team, you need to go to the team meetings; you need to be a part of the discussion about how a church is "running the plays" of outreach in the community. You are for the church! You have a place and a role in a local congregation, and to argue that you don't have to go to church to be part of the church might be true—but is it right?

> *But now indeed there are many members, yet one body. And the eye cannot say to the hand, "I have no need of you"; nor again the head to the feet, "I have no need of you.*
>
> — 1 CORINTHIANS 12:20-21 (NKJV)

You and I are part of the *global* body of believers that is called the church, but you also have something to contribute to a *local* congregation, and just as no one can tell you that you're not needed in church, neither can you say that you don't need church. Yes, you may be a student of the Word, and, yes, you may be faithful at witnessing and sharing your faith, and these things are good! But your gifts and talents are also needed at the local church. Isolation is never a solution when Fractured Fellowship has occurred. It's bad for the individual, and it's bad for the church. One reason I say this is because we have the "Instructions for Conflict Resolution" in the Word of God, and when the steps are followed as outlined out in Matthew 18, then a positive outcome and restoration become possible. If they are ignored, then it remains impossible.

With that said, I'll be the first to admit that pastors and church leaders hurt people; but I must also say that hurting people often hurt people, and the act of leaving a church should be preceded by much prayer and examination of facts vs. feelings. This is what I mean: I've often said that churches are like toast. Some people like theirs plain, some with butter, others with butter and jelly. If your decision to Fracture Fellowship and leave a local church is a matter of taste, then leave it at that. Don't look for things to justify your departure or someone to blame. If you don't like the pastor's style, if the worship style isn't your thing, that's ok. There's room for personal taste in choosing a church, but be careful about labeling worship or preaching styles as sinful when you search for a church. If you're sensing the need to go, then you must also ask if your decision is facts-based or feelings-based.

Leaving a church over matters of taste and preference isn't really Fractured Fellowship, but it's often treated as though it were. Just to let you into a pastor's head for a minute, one thing that immediately sends up a red flag for me when meeting someone new at the church is when they start telling me everything that was wrong at their old one. (By the way, I don't allow them to do this, and I just tell them I'm glad they've joined us for the day.) The vast majority of the time, whatever their reasons for departure (which I usually pick up on before I end the conversation), it was usually a matter of taste—not fact—and they're angry. I have to say that most of the time, when I've done something that's hurt a fellow believer or when something happened that has hurt me, it was *the way* things were done and not *what* was done that actually caused the hurt.

But what if the truth is that something *did* happen? A legitimate wrong was committed that wasn't a matter of personal taste, hurt feelings, or opinion. What happens then? Two things to consider:

> Moreover if your brother sins against you, go and tell him his fault between you and him alone. If he hears you, you have gained your brother. But if he will not hear, take with you one or two more, that "by the mouth of two or three witnesses every word may be established." And if he refuses to hear them, tell it to the church. But if he refuses even to hear the church, let him be to you like a heathen and a tax collector.
>
> — MATTHEW 18:15-17 (NKJV)

There are multiple lessons here, and the first and foremost is that God desires for problems to be handled with the fewest number of people involved as possible. Go to the one who committed a *biblically defined sin*—not just something that hurt your feelings, not just something that's different from your tastes or opinions, but something that the Bible has defined as a sin. Go to them the first time by yourself. I believe that the reason this progression is given is in recognition of human nature. Some people believe everything they hear and are quick to repeat it, which causes unnecessary harm to the persons and to the church. If a sin has been committed against you, go to the person first—not the church first (meaning to others that you know). Let me also say this: I believe that it's good to seek counsel from a mature brother or sister in the Lord before doing this, just to make sure that the situation is one of facts and not feelings.

If they won't hear you, take others who are mature in the Lord and aware of the sin and confront them. If they still won't hear, Fractured Fellowship is then not only unavoidable but is mandated. As I said a moment ago, sometimes the person who committed the sin is one in leadership or even behind the pulpit. In an age where the public failures of prominent pastors isn't all that uncommon, we need to add one more element to making the decision to Fracture Fellowship with your church or church leader:

> Do not receive an accusation against an elder except from two or three witnesses. Those who are sinning rebuke in the presence of all, that the rest also may fear.
>
> — 1 TIMOTHY 5:19-20 (NKJV)

I believe that this instruction is a word of caution. Just as with King David when he sinned with Bathsheba against her husband, Uriah, the fall of a church leader gives occasion for the enemies of God to blaspheme. If a legitimate sin has been committed against you by a church leader, don't let their fall lead to your own! They failed; God did not. They sinned against you; God did not. They owe you an apology; God does not. You still owe Him your very life, and human failures can never diminish the goodness of God.

We've talked about the "why" questions in previous chapters, and Fractured Fellowship causes them also, but in this case, we have the answer, and that is: God uses fallible human beings as leaders in His church because He has no other resources from which to draw! Every pastor, every church leader, every Sunday school teacher, has the capacity to fail and to hurt others, and God is responsible for none of it.

> ## It just doesn't make sense to give up on God when humans fail.

Many years ago, I had signed up to be a follow-up counselor at a large evangelistic outreach and was very nervous, as it was my first time doing anything like that. As the event wrapped up and those who had made commitments to the Lord were being paired up with counselors, I was assigned to a young woman with two small children. What followed is etched in my mind forever. I introduced myself by saying, "Hi, my name is Barry," to which the woman burst into tears and began to weep so loudly that it scared her kids and attracted the attention of the field supervisor who was nearby.

When the woman got control of her emotions, she said, "I've been having an affair with a pastor, and I had to recommit my life to the Lord tonight and repent—and his name is [you guessed it,] Barry!" (It wasn't me!) This was why the woman burst into tears when I introduced myself: she'd been hurt by someone who should have protected her and not taken advantage of her vulnerability, and now, here she was, deeply wounded—and by a church leader.

This is the type of scenario that we're considering: when church leaders commit sins against the very people they're supposed to protect. It is certainly not limited to the sexual realm, but this seems to be the most frequently publicized failure of church leaders.

So what now? A biblically identified sin has been committed, and the biblical model for confrontation has been followed, yet whether or not repentance has happened, the wound is there. How do you move forward? How do you Dance with this Scar? We've already discussed the need to distance this from God, for He is incapable of sin and isn't the initiator or tempter with evil (James 1:13). The second thing to note is much like in our opening chapter, where we learned that you have to get moving again and reengage in a church community. I've heard time and again people say things like: "I've been hurt by the church too many times! I just don't want to go through that again."

My hurting friend, Fractured Fellowship hurts, but you have to move ahead as a part of the body. You, like those in our first two chapters, must get back into the flow of things as a member of the church, and this is going to expose you to the possibility of getting hurt by the fallible folks who attend every church.

> And let us consider one another in order to stir up
> love and good works, not forsaking the assembling
> of ourselves together, as is the manner of some,

*but exhorting one another, and so much the more
as you see the Day approaching.*

— HEBREWS 10:24-25 (NKJV)

No matter how you slice it, Hebrews 10:25 tells us:
"Go to church! Don't forsake the assembling with other
believers." Some argue that this doesn't mean the church
corporate, as we know it; but yes, it does! It means exactly
that. The Greek word for "assembly" is *episynagōgē*: epi,
meaning "upon," and synagoge is where we derive our
word "synagogue," which speaks of the physical gather-
ing place for worship and study of the Word. The Book of
Hebrews says that we're not to forsake "synagogue-ing"
ourselves together, as some do. Some of the angriest and
most bitter people that I have ever met are those who've
been hurt by someone in the church, yet they are still
closer to the cure for anger and bitterness than anyone
who is in the world. But like so many other things that
hurt us, the lack of justice or acknowledgment by the perpetrator leaves them wounded, and they never get around
to Dancing with the Scars.

There was a time when I had come under attack for
a long period of time from another pastor. He had lied
about me, had hurt my family deeply, and had damaged
relationships that I had with people, through the lies and
innuendoes with which he targeted me. This was a long
and deep valley for my wife and me, and I was baffled
at why the Lord hadn't done anything and had allowed
it to continue. I sustained a deep and bitter wound, as

this man had once been my close friend. There was a day when I prayed, asking God for the umpteenth time why He continued to allow this man to get away with what he was doing. I heard a voice inside my head and heart say, "I didn't. I've heard and seen everything."

I share this with you for this reason: This is what we are really after when someone who should be a trusted Christian leader hurts us—or when anyone hurts us, for that matter: recognition. We need acknowledgement that a wrong has been committed against us and for that to be recognized by others.

> God is saying to you who have experienced Fractured Fellowship caused by a church leader, "I saw it all, and I recognize that it hurt you."

I have to tell you that those words truly set me free from the wounds I had received from this man and it allowed them to become scars. No more prayers for justice, no more longing for someone to come to me and say, "I knew what he said wasn't true." To remember that God hears and sees all, that I matter, and that He cares about me is what I really needed. Yes, the damage that this man has done has impacted relationships that I once enjoyed, and to this day, these are the scars that I still live with. I don't know if there will ever be reconciliation or ownership on his part, but that's between Him and the Lord. I'm free!

This is going to be true for most of you who have been wounded by church leaders. You will have to reengage in the church, accepting the fact that no one ever gets away with anything as God's child. We can't get hung up on the fact that the person who sinned against us is still in the ministry or hasn't yet been disciplined by the Lord. If the sin was criminal, that's a different story. But if a leader lied about you, committed sexual sin, or any other biblically identified sins, you need to follow the guidelines set by Jesus in Matthew 18, and if the church leadership does nothing, know that God saw it all, and He will act in His time.

When this man was attacking me, he was also hurting others, and many of them knew what he had done to me and asked me, innocently, to lead a campaign against him. I was not going to become a Christian vigilante, even though my flesh wanted to join the strike team, and I told the group who had come to me that the Lord would take care of the matter, which He did.

Consider the words of Jesus to the church at Thyatira in Revelation 2:

> *Nevertheless I have a few things against you, because you allow that woman Jezebel, who calls herself a prophetess, to teach and seduce My servants to commit sexual immorality and eat things sacrificed to idols. And I gave her time to repent of her sexual immorality, and she did not repent.*

Indeed I will cast her into a sickbed, and those who commit adultery with her into great tribulation, unless they repent of their deeds.

— REVELATION 2:20-22 (NKJV)

I'm glad that God hasn't treated me the way that I've wished He would treat others at times.

(And fortunately for others, God does what is right and not what I ask!) I'm glad that He gives time for sinners to repent, even of sexual immorality, before He acts. It may be that the one who hurt you is in just such a season—and, again, let me be clear: when a person's safety or moral purity is at stake, decisive action must be taken. We've had to take such a position in our church and have had to report people to the authorities for their actions outside of the church. I say this because it's become en vogue to accuse the church of orchestrating cover-ups, and, in some cases, it's true. But God sees and knows all, and all things are naked and open before His sight.

Another issue that often surfaces in the church that causes Fractured Fellowship is "position seeking." At times, those who desire leadership positions in the church, which is neither wrong nor bad, resort to ladder-climbing tactics as if the church has a corporate ladder to climb and only the strong survive and advance. Two words of counsel in this area:

A man's gift makes room for him,
And brings him before great men.

— PROVERBS 18:16 (NKJV)

Let another man praise you, and
not your own mouth;
A stranger, and not your own lips.

— PROVERBS 27:2 (NKJV)

Ladder climbing, positioning, and posturing in the church is wrong. Desiring to be used by God is right and good, and the Lord calls and equips us all for His own will and purposes. The gifts that He gives will open the right doors—in His time—and self-promotion is unnecessary and even harmful in the body of Christ, largely because…

Building oneself up usually involves
tearing someone else down.

Yet it happens, even in the church, and maybe even to you.

So what now? Someone has used you as a rung on the church leadership ladder and has left you discouraged and wounded. Do you fracture fellowship and look for another church? This is a huge decision that requires much prayer and seeking of wisdom, as church families are often more intimate than blood families, and when that is taken away, disillusionment and despair can sometimes dominate thoughts and emotions.

Let me first address this through a series of questions that you can ask yourself. The first one is the most important: *Is this God's will?* I believe that the congregant is just as "called" to a particular church as is the pastor: although their roles in making the church operate may be different, both are necessary and important. It takes fingers, hands, arms, knees, and toes to make the body function properly, and each of us has a role in a local church. So when the aspiring church leader or co-worker has inflicted wounds from which there seem to be no relief, and the decision is made to move on and find another church, the first and most important consideration is what God wants. God asks us to do the hard thing sometimes. He asks us to stick it out when we feel like bailing out.

How do you know if God is calling you to move on? Ask yourself if you've finished what He called you to do in the first place. Is the task complete? The vision fulfilled? The mission accomplished? These questions are important to ask because church ladder-climbers and position seekers cannot be allowed to thwart the will of God in your life by getting you to bail out on your calling. They are always going to be there, and changing churches won't change that.

I've had numerous people over the years who, on their first, and usually only, Sunday at our church, offered to preach for me should I be gone or need a week off. My answer is always, "Thank you for the offer, but I have a group of trusted and faithful men already to whom I look for that." It seems to offend them that upon our first meeting

I don't count them among that group—but that's on them, not me. Before moving on from your church home, make sure that the ministry to which you were called isn't going to be hurt because of it and that God has released you from what you had committed to do for Him.

What are the signs that fracturing fellowship might actually be in order? First of all, please understand that we are dealing with people-stuff here, and not legal or moral issues. I actually often wish that fractured fellowship would take place because the teaching is heretical or the leadership immoral. Too many saints sit under such things for far too long sometimes. Taking those things off the table, and considering that you may be in a good church under godly leadership, but there is that person who has wounded you, and you are certain that emotions are not what's driving you, what do you do? You're convinced that you've "fulfilled your calling and ministry" and that God isn't telling you to finish the task at hand— or maybe your involvement wasn't that much anyway. So what do you do?

How do you know if it's the right thing to do? Here is the first thing to consider: Is what happened in this situation hindering your ability to receive from the teaching at the church? Do you sit through the sermon, thinking only about what happened to you and wondering why no one has done anything about it or seems to even see it? Have you, "as much as depends on you," sought peace? You may be thinking, *But I didn't do anything wrong! Why should I seek peace?*

The answer is simple and not meant to sound trite, but it's true: you should seek peace because you're the one who is living without it. When you find yourself no longer able to receive from the teaching—and you've sought to make peace—it may be time for you to move on and away from that person. The other reason that seeking peace is important is because it informs the other person that you were offended, and should you ever come to the place where being in another church family is what is best, you won't have to enter your new church thinking, *Why didn't I say something? Maybe things could have worked out.* You will be less likely to have to bring the hurts and bitter feelings with you. Fractured Fellowship is painful and hard, and it should be. The old adage, "You only hurt the ones you love," is the reason for that. The church is to be known by its *love for one another*, and Fractured Fellowship reveals the church's failure in this area (unless heresy or clear sin is involved).

I know that many people today change churches like they change clothes, and that's wrong.

> Many have heard the saying, "Grow where you're planted." Let me add to that, "You can't grow until you're planted!"

Grow in your relationships with other believers in service to the Lord as an active and contributing part of a local band of believers serving the community. There are certain aspects of the Christian experience that happen and are fulfilled by being part of the assembly of believers that we refer to as the church.

Should you come to the place where it's time for you to move to a different meeting location, let me add this: Do not do so launching grenades as you leave. I've learned that at times God has to use things like this to get us out of our comfort zones and into the next season of His will for our lives. Sometimes, the only way that He can get us out of our comfort zones is by making those zones *uncomfortable*. But handle this with great care, as you would any family situation. Do it with love in your mind and hope for resolution in your heart. If you do these things, and reconciliation is still impossible, you can move to your next assignment with peace of mind, even though with pain in your heart.

I wish that I had the words that might make the scar of Fractured Fellowship go away for some of you, but that will have to wait until Heaven. For now, you and I will have to move forward bearing the battle scars of being part of a church with a perfect Head and an imperfect body. Let your wound scar over, and don't let the devil trick you into blaming God or the whole church for the actions of a few. Find a Bible-teaching church with a good and godly pastor, and serve the Lord there and in your personal life. Good and godly pastors aren't as rare as you may think. Perhaps they're not as "high profile" as some, but even they are fallible humans who may hurt people once in a while.

Don't blame God for what people do—even Christian people. One of the devil's favorite tactics is isolation, but remember: you need the church, and the church needs you! If you're thinking, *I'm doing fine without being part of a church*, then you're making my point, because being part of the church should be something that we desire—not despise. Also, keep in mind that God sees and knows all, and vengeance and discipline are His. Maybe the one who has hurt you is in the time-to-repent season that we ourselves would desire from the Lord if we were the "hurter" and not the "hurt-ee."

God is on the throne, Christian, and not any church leader. He is sovereign and it is His will that you be a part of a church family that meets collectively for the purpose of finding out what is acceptable to the Lord and being equipped for the work of ministry.

"I can do that without going to church," you say?

> Now you are the body of Christ, and members individually. And God has appointed these in the church: first apostles, second prophets, third teachers, after that miracles, then gifts of healings, helps, administrations, varieties of tongues. Are all apostles? Are all prophets? Are all teachers? Are all workers of miracles? Do all have gifts of healings? Do all speak with tongues? Do all interpret? But earnestly desire the best gifts. And yet I show you a more excellent way.
>
> — 1 CORINTHIANS 12:27-31 (NKJV)

It takes all of these gifts and "appointments" to make the church function, including administrations, which means governance. This enables the church to function as it should, with each part doing its share—and it's all to be done in the "more excellent way," which is found in the next chapter, and that is *love*.

God has a plan for you—not just as a member of His vast global church, but He has works that He prepared beforehand for *you* to walk in as a functioning member of a local assembly of believers in order for that assembly to function fully within the community that God has called and assigned them to reach. Don't let the boneheads in the body keep you from walking in your gifts and fulfilling your ministry!

Someday, when we are glorified and the former things have passed away, we won't have to deal with hurting one another or being hurt ever again! But until then, we are a collective group of personality types, with ambitions and methods that can get a little fleshly at times—and even a *lot* fleshly for some. So remember whom it is you serve, for He has never hurt you, stabbed you in the back, lied about you, tried to climb over you, walked by you without speaking, or done any of the things to you that cause Fractured Fellowship. Faulty human beings have been responsible for them all, and they attend every church and even pastor them also. Where heresy and immorality are clearly present, run for your life. Where wounds with the potential to Fracture Fellowship occur, choose the more excellent way, even when it's time to move on.

10

All Things?

As we come to our final chapter, there's a truth we need to address that is a fitting conclusion to Dancing with the Scars, no matter their source. Whether it's the loss of a loved one, the violence of divorce, the betrayal of a friend, or any of the topics that we've discussed in previous chapters, there's one thing they all have in common: well-meaning people say well-intended things that either aggravate the wound or that seem insensitive, considering the circumstances. We've all done it, and most of those who have experienced a life wound have experienced it.

Here's an example of what I'm talking about: A person has lost a loved one, and someone who genuinely cares asks them how they're doing. The person on the receiving end wants to scream, "How do you *think* I'm doing? I'm doing awful! I just lost my child (or spouse, parent or sibling)!" But the one in pain is generally kind and receives the well-meant inquiry with grace, saying that they are hanging in there (or some other expected response). I can think back to a few times when I've wished that I could reel in my words when offering condolences to a suffering person, even though they were well-meant but poorly chosen.

The most common among those statements expressed to people at a time of loss or injury is a well-known verse from Romans, which, while true, is often poorly timed when offered:

> And we know that all things work together for good to those who love God, to those who are the called according to His purpose.
>
> — ROMANS 8:28 (NKJV)

The day of the trauma or tragedy is *not* the time to be sharing such a verse. The suffering person's mind is reeling with shock as a defense mechanism to protect the brain from sensory overload. This is also not the right verse to share at the funeral with someone who is grieving, or on the day the layoff notice comes, or when the heart is trying to survive betrayal, having been broken into a thousand pieces. Think about saying, "All things work together for good" to the parents of a stillborn child or the spouse of a murder victim. It doesn't fit the moment, but it does beg the question: What does *"all things"* mean? Can it possibly apply to the aforementioned scenarios?

Does "all things" include even *those* things? The answer
is yes—but with an explanation.

First of all, we need to understand what Romans 8:28
is *not* saying. It is not saying that the loss of a loved one or
the ending of a marriage or the consequences of friendly
fire are actually "good things." What Romans is actually
saying is:

> When life is at its worst, when pain
> and wounds are the deepest, God can do
> something in you that is good.

Like what? you may be thinking. *What possible good
can God do in me when I've lost my child or mate? What
good can come from betrayal or abandonment?* The first
thing to note is that there are some things in which there
will never be any good while we are "in" them, but there
can be good that comes *through* them. Nothing we've
discussed in any of the previous chapters can be seen as
"good." I must say, however, that I would not even hazard
a guess as to how many times these very scenarios have
led to our seeing the goodness of God being manifested
in someone's life. I've seen His goodness manifested in
the lives of people who have endured great trauma and
tragedy, yet they reacted with strength and a peace that
passes understanding. I have seen people betrayed and
abandoned who've displayed the goodness of God by forgiving the unforgivable and displaying grace and mercy to
the degree that none could deny that God's goodness was

showing through them. I have seen more people that I can count who've had their personal traumas turned into ministries, and while there never was and never will be any good "in" the circumstances they've endured, good did come *from* them, in that they were able to use their traumatic situation as the voice of experience, offering others counsel in ways that no one else could.

This is how the All Things of Romans 8:28 must be understood and embraced when Life Happens, and Wounds and Scars are created. There is also a point that we need to note concerning chapter 2 and Wounds and Scars, and that is:

> All wounds create scars, but there
> are different kinds of scars.

In that chapter, I mentioned a wound that I acquired in third grade and the scar that was left on my knee as a result. That's an old wound, and the scar now has no feeling. It's visible but not painful. I have also had three surgeries, including nerve surgery, on my right elbow, the last one about thirty years ago. That scar is far different from the one on my knee, as it's still tender to this day and is very sensitive when I bump it against something, so I'm still protective and conscious of it even though the surgery was so long ago. The point is this: transitioning from wound to scar doesn't mean you'll have a pain-free existence, and although time may lessen the memory, and the scar fades, it may still be painful when bumped. In truth, the concept of "All Things" that we're talking about, which results in good, doesn't necessarily mean that we'll have a pain-free existence on the other side of the trauma.

Let me illustrate this through personal experience. I found myself a bit surprised recently when speaking at a conference and sharing Teri's and my story. What happened as I spoke had happened before, but I wasn't expecting it this time for two reasons: the event had happened a long time ago, and I had shared it so often that I didn't think the emotions that sometimes presented themselves in the past would emerge in this moment. But I found myself fighting to control my emotions and hold back my tears when I shared that during Teri's and my separation I had missed my daughter's second birthday. For me, this is a reminder of the epic failure in my past life. I have others that are equal, or greater, that I will never use as examples because those scars are not ones I'm willing to share.

What I want you to see is this: I was ministering while still hurting. My wound was self-inflicted, while yours may not be, but the principle remains unchanged. We can carry with us scars that are still sensitive and painful, even though we can see the good of ministering to others manifested through our lives.

The matter of timing is critical concerning all things working together for good, as we made the point about the timing of even sharing such a verse. The point of the last paragraph was that you don't have to wait for the pain to be completely gone before you can begin to look for the good that God wants to do or to reveal through you.

You're going to have scars in life that are faded and pain-less memories, and there will be others that hurt no matter how much time passes.

My wife and I were having breakfast one morning not too long ago, and the subject came up of our two children who are in Heaven due to miscarried pregnancies. We'd never really talked about it before, and I asked Teri if she ever thinks about seeing those children in Heaven. She replied that she thinks about them every day! We wept together over this 35-plus-year-old loss. What good came from this? For one thing, when we weep with those who weep, we gain deeper compassion and understanding. Thus, when this trauma impacts the lives of others, we can share with them our expectation of meeting children whom we've never seen when we arrive in Heaven. (And yes—this means that I believe that life begins at concep-tion! Because it does.) The point is that for you to begin to look for the good that can come through something doesn't have to correspond with your pain level. I do think that caution must be exercised in this area, because some try to jump right back into things too soon and never really allow themselves time to grieve.

A few moments ago I brought up having missed my daughter's second birthday. I mentioned this for two rea-sons: 1) to illustrate the difference in kinds of scars and 2) to address the issue of ministering with those scars, i.e., seeing good come *through* them. This isn't a blan-ket truth, and it's not possible with all scars or with all people. It may be that some things are painful memories that will never turn into ministries. I have things in my life, as I said, that are better just left behind. I haven't asked God to use them, nor do I want Him to, for they are far too painful and disgusting to repeat. In the same way, not every sexually abused person will have that painful remembrance become an area of ministry—at least not publicly—and it's okay if it never does. You can still minister by empathy and intercessory prayer when you hear of such situations, or if you know someone who's been hurt similarly by others. No one can pray for the pain of others like someone who has shared the same experience; no one can know the deep agony of the loss of a child like someone who has lost one; no one understands the aloneness and despair that comes from divorce as well as those who've been through it—and for some, the subject is too painful to talk about publicly.

My point is that I don't want anyone to feel guilty because they haven't taken their testimony on a speaking tour and gone public with everything that's happened to them. You can still exhibit the goodness of God through your circumstances by the compassion that you show to others who may be walking in your shoes.

> The good that can be manifested through
> what you've experienced may be less visible,
> but it is no less valuable.

I must also say that although the words that we're discussing here from Romans may have been shared with you in an untimely manner, the fact that you're reading a book with such a title may indicate that now is the right time for you to hear them! Maybe now is the time to acknowledge that there's still good to be found in life in spite of what you've endured and that you may even come through it a stronger person!

> *For it is the God who commanded light to shine out of darkness, who has shone in our hearts to give the light of the knowledge of the glory of God in the face of Jesus Christ. But we have this treasure in earthen vessels, that the excellence of the power may be of God and not of us. We are hard-pressed on every side, yet not crushed; we are perplexed, but not in despair; persecuted, but not forsaken; struck down, but not destroyed —* *always carrying about in the body the dying of the Lord Jesus, that the life of Jesus also may be manifested in our body. For we who live are always delivered to death for Jesus' sake, that the life of Jesus also may be manifested in our mortal flesh.*
>
> — 2 CORINTHIANS 4:6-11 (NKJV)

Paul travels in some pretty elite spiritual company, in my mind, and is paired with men like Joseph and Job when it comes to dealing with life's traumas and tribulations. Yet Paul, like Joseph and Job, seemed to understand the "All Things" principle in a way that was made visible to others both in word and deed.

The next thing I want to point out is packaged in a way that makes it easy to remember:

Problems do not change your purpose.

We could insert "trials," "traumas," "tribulations"—any number of descriptive terms or phrases that would all be fitting, but the all-encompassing description of these things as "problems" not only lends itself to being remembered but also covers all the bases. This is what Paul is saying here through his comparative phrases: "hard-pressed, but not crushed; perplexed, but not in despair; persecuted, but not forsaken; struck down, but not destroyed." I want to remind you that you, too, can travel in this elite crowd! You can say, as Joseph did to his betraying brothers:

> But as for you, you meant evil against me; but God meant it for good, in order to bring it about as it is this day, to save many people alive.
> — GENESIS 50:20 (NKJV)

Joseph's circumstances were these: his jealous brothers sold him into slavery to a traveling merchant, and during his captivity, the wife of a high-ranking official cast her eyes upon him. When he refused her advances, she accused him of assaulting her, and he was imprisoned. While in prison, he interpreted the dreams of two other prisoners concerning their futures: one was executed and the other released, just as Joseph had said. Joseph asked the man who was about to be set free, "Remember me, and see if you can get me out of here, because I'm innocent of all charges." But when the man resumed his former position in the kingdom, he forgot about his promise to Joseph for two years. Joseph was finally released from prison and, through a series of circumstances, was promoted to second-in-command in all of Egypt! After all these things and with many years passing, his brothers, who had been the cause of this whole situation, found themselves standing before their brother Joseph, asking for food in the midst of a seven-year famine. What you just read in the above verse was Joseph's reply to them once they realized who he was.

That is what "hard-pressed on every side, yet not crushed; perplexed, but not in despair; persecuted, but not forsaken; struck down, but not destroyed" looks like in the life of someone who understands the All Things principle. Problems, in whatever way that word may be defined for you, never change the purpose of your existence as a Christian. The problem may change you, it may change your circumstances, it may change your happiness, it may change your pain level, it may change your ability to trust certain people, it may require you to forgive certain people for your own sake—but your *purpose* will never change, which is to be a light that shines out of darkness: to be a witness, to love and serve God, to meet the needs around us as we are able, to recognize that the evil meant against us may not really come from family but from powers and principalities and rulers of darkness in this age (Ephesians 6:12).

So as you begin to move forward in an effort to Dance with the Scars, remember that as a Christian you are one of the called according to His purpose. You will have to move forward with unanswered questions, especially the "why" question in cases of life trauma, betrayal, divorce, and unforeseen circumstances. You will have to recognize that you cannot live life with a continual open wound. As the phases of grief are encountered, make sure that you are progressing toward acceptance, which begins with leaning on God and not blaming Him, remembering that what is true about Him in good times is still true when things are tragic or tough.

You must also recognize that although people who have experienced trauma find themselves with many counselors, the timing and stages of grief are different for each person, and denial and anger can rear their heads multiple times on the journey toward acceptance. For those who have been told that they should pick themselves up and move forward as though grief were a sin for a child of God, remember: wounds create scars on Christians just as they do on anyone else. Life happens in ways that hurt and create painful memories that can even interfere with someone's thought processes. God can and does heal and restore—in His time, not other people's.

Remember that we're engaged in spiritual warfare, and the devil doesn't let up just because we're wounded. He will try to create confusion and doubt that lead to fear and despair, and we must never exchange what we *don't* know for what we *do* know. We don't know why God allows the things that He does, but we do know that He is good—all the time. We don't know why God heals some and not others during this life, but we do know that every Christian has an eternal, pain-free existence awaiting them. The enemy wants to see you live the rest of your life in wound care, and he'll do all he can to inhibit your ever Dancing with the Scars. He'll kick you when you're down, aggravate your wound, and he'll often use the people around you to do it. He loves it when friendly fire separates families and friends—nothing pleases him more than to ruin a once-loving and close relationship by inspiring misconceptions and inconsiderate words. It's during such times that we must remember that we're not defined by the words or perceptions of others. We are defined by the Word of God!

We also must engage in the very difficult task of recognizing that not everything that hurts us is bad for us, and the method or the messenger who has offended us may actually have said things that were true. We need to remember that Proverbs 29:11 says that it is foolish to speak all that's in your heart, and sometimes being silent in return is the right thing, even if nothing that was said against us was right or even true! That doesn't mean that we should never defend ourselves against verbal assaults, but there are times when we need to let God be our defense. The truth is there are times when *only* He can be our defense—for example, when what He has joined together has been ripped apart like two napkins once glued together, leaving a bit of each on the other when the one become two. When a Christian encounters the violence of divorce, and a life is turned upside down, with everything changing dramatically for one or the other—frequently more so for the wife, who is thrust into the position of being the sole provider—isolation becomes more dangerous and fellowship more important than ever.

Divorce is not something to be treated flippantly or as if it were a societal norm. It hurts people deeply. It often wounds the innocent and unaware, it impacts children, it breaks hearts, it damages people and culture. Those who have endured this great trauma need to remember that they have an identity that is separate from that of being married—an identity in Christ, who never leaves us nor forsakes us, who is never abusive or adulterous, who is the very definition of faithfulness in all things. It is that identity that reminds us to be Spirit-led Christians even when walking through the valley of the shadow of the death of a marriage. God has a plan for you as an individual member of the collective body of Christ, and your life is not over because your marriage has ended. There are still good works prepared beforehand for you to walk in (Ephesians 2:10)!

Maybe your wounds weren't from the loss of a loved one, from friendly fire, or the aftermath of divorce. Maybe you've caused your own wounds. Maybe you're dealing with the consequences of forgiven sin. The possibility of Dancing with the Scars is just as much a reality for you as anyone else. It will take some discipline in your thinking to arrive there, however, including recognizing that the past will always be present in our hearts, but it need not rule the present in our minds. Some self-inflicted wounds will create lifelong scars in the form of broken relationships, lost trust, and other various consequences, all continuing to be felt even though the sin has been completely forgiven. Reconciliation for self-inflicted wounds is a good thing to pursue. We must remember that the person who caused the broken relationship doesn't set the terms for restoring the relationship. Trust has to be earned, and even forgiven actions can have consequences on the interpersonal relationship level. Be careful about having a sense of entitlement, which indicates that you may not understand what forgiveness really means. Forgiveness can come *without* the restoration of the relationship happening. It doesn't have to be that way, but sometimes, it just is.

Some may be thinking that All Things can't possibly include "what happened to me as a child—the sexual, emotional, or physical abuse that was endured." Yes, All Things includes those things, if we remember that there is a freedom that comes from forgiving others. Forgiveness doesn't mean we act as though nothing ever happened. Forgiveness is often beneficial primarily for the forgiver rather than for the forgiven. Those who are trying to learn to dance with such scars will have to accept that what happened can never be made right. This is essential, because these areas trap more people in wound care for long periods than any of the others.

It's natural for us to want justice and acknowledgement when someone has greatly or brutally wronged us. It is a sad reality that most of the time victims of life-altering incidents rarely have their sense of justice satisfied for various reasons. Still, Dancing with the Scars is possible and is going to require recognizing that even justice will not remove the memories or pain. The need for justice is strong, and to know that it may never come can be disheartening, but at some point, we've all observed the public forgiveness offered to someone who killed another's loved one[s], and the reality is that *forgiveness can do more for the broken heart and mind than justice will ever do!* There is a justice that will be served in the end for all who do not believe in Jesus and repent of their sins, and we are not to wish that justice upon our worst enemies.

All Things also includes the 3 Ds we mentioned in chapter 7: Disappointment, Discouragement, and Despair when life didn't follow the course that we had mapped out: the business venture didn't pan out, the childhood dreams of sports stardom never materialized, or whatever we hoped would happen as an adult...didn't. The first step in dealing with dashed hopes and unrealized dreams is to get new ones—even spiritual ones!

Dream of doing great things for God, which is always more rewarding, and even more likely, than following our personal dreams anyway. The truth is that when we tap into God's plans, we aren't limited to our natural abilities and are assured of supernatural help. "God has a great plan for your life"—this is not just a Christian mantra; it's true! He has plans for you, and they are great. Think about it: does God have any mediocre plans? He is able to, and does do, above and beyond what we ask or think

(Ephesians 3:20). So in this area, more than the others, we have the choice to either stall out in disappointment, discouragement, and despair, or we can say, "God, my plans didn't work out. What are yours?" All Things includes all of the things that we have dreamed and desired that never came to fruition. It's not that it was bad to dream them, or wrong to dream them, but not all dreams come true. Here's some good news, though: God's plans do!

Unforeseen circumstances that bring about a change of lifestyle financially also fall under the All Things umbrella. This difficult scenario requires some mental adjustments as well, in the form of a few reminders, one being: *Contentment comes from God, not from things.* Paul told Timothy that "godliness with contentment is great gain" (1 Timothy 6:6), and the sense of contentment often flees when unforeseen circumstances have a financial impact. Established contentment is the target goal, and it makes the point that discontentment is learned behavior. We know this because there are impoverished people all over the world who, though they would like a change of financial circumstance, are still content and joyful people because they understand that godliness is great gain. It's easy for us to say, when we encounter an economic downturn, that we lost everything. That isn't true, and we need to remember that of all we once did have, the Lord gave us the strength to earn it in the first place, and all that we still have is actually His. This kind of thinking will help us to avoid having a financial downturn become a spiritual one. Job knew a bit about losing it all, and his conclusion was, "The Lord gave, and the Lord has taken away; Blessed be the name of the Lord. In all this Job did not sin nor charge God with wrong" (Job 1:22).

Yes, even a financial downturn can work together for good, but we have to let God define "good" and let go of our human definitions.

We can also rightly place the sad but true reality of fractured fellowship in the All Things category. Whether fractured fellowship ought to happen or is completely avoidable is irrelevant for our causes, because it does happen. Pastors and parishioners, leaders and layman, hurt one another, and much of it is definitely miscommunication or misunderstanding—but not all of it. Some is pride and ego. No matter which side of the pulpit or lectern you may be on, don't blame God for what people have done. Remember, the thief comes only to steal, kill, and destroy (John 10:10), and the more he can divide the church, the more he steals, kills, and destroys the unity of the Spirit. He hates the church and everyone in it. He loves discord among the brethren because God hates it. The more of it that he can cause, the more pleased he is.

This is why the Lord has given us clear-cut instructions about how to deal with our differences. Every pastor, every church leader, every Sunday school teacher, has the capacity to fail and hurt others, and God is responsible for none of it. Yet, because they fail, many fracture fellowship with their church or even have a crisis of faith. But remember: It just doesn't make sense to give up on God when humans fail.

Jesus said that the world would know that we are His disciples by the love that we have for one another (John 13:35). I wonder what the world thinks about the church when they see fractured fellowship? Jesus' statement implies that their conclusion will be that we are more like them than like Him. God allows us time to repent—of sin. We have to make sure that feelings, emotions, and opinions are not causing fractured fellowship and that an actual I-can-find-it-in-the-Bible sin has been committed and that the process for dealing with it, as lined out in Matthew 18 by Jesus, is followed. I think that most of you could agree when I say, "I'm glad that God hasn't treated me the way that I've wished He treated others at times." The best may not always be true, but thinking the best is where our mind should start until proven otherwise. And yes, All Things, including fractured fellowship, can work together for the good of the called according to His purpose. It is good when biblical discipline is followed, and it is good when restoration of a sinning brother or sister occurs. The guidelines must be followed to the letter to see the good come out of fractured fellowship.

I want to conclude our "dance lesson" with a couple of closing thoughts. We've talked candidly about some hard things: things that our flesh will instantly reject, things that our emotions will resist, things that we will have a hard time getting our head around, specifically, moving forward without closure. It may feel like that, and your mind and emotions may be robbed initially of what you feel they need to move on, but *moving forward is closure.* The truth is you have to want it, and you have to believe it, because we will never have or do what we don't fully believe. If you aren't convinced that it's possible for All Things to include whatever you've endured or encountered in life, then Dancing with the Scars will remain an illusive dream and not a present reality. You'll have to push forward, and with some pains, but you must believe that the biblical phrase that I paraphrased to arrive at our title is true—for you.

> *You have turned my mourning into joyful dancing. You have taken away my clothes of mourning and clothed me with joy, that I might sing praises to you and not be silent. O LORD my God, I will give you thanks forever!*
>
> — PSALM 30:11-12 (NLT)

Your mourning can turn into dancing, and you can be clothed with joy! It will be a joy that bears some scars, with some more tender than others, but your destiny in life doesn't have to be among the walking wounded, no matter what the wound was or when it occurred.

Is it going to be easy? No. Will it be worth it? Yes! I have filled this book with Scripture, because I believe what Isaiah 55:11 says, that God's Word will not return void, not even when the reader is you! You can Dance with the Scars, you can be clothed with joy. "It's going to take a miracle," you say? That's exactly what we've been talking about all along. A miracle that is possible through the God of the Bible who does miracles! But you have to want it, and you have to believe it.

It doesn't just end there, however, and the closing reminder for you comes from the words of Jesus Himself:

> *But why do you call Me "Lord, Lord," and not do the things which I say? Whoever comes to Me, and hears My sayings and does them, I will show you whom he is like: He is like a man building a house, who dug deep and laid the foundation on the rock. And when the flood arose, the stream beat vehemently against that house, and could not shake it, for it was founded on the rock. But he who heard and did nothing is like a man who built a house on the earth without a foundation, against which the stream beat vehemently; and immediately it fell. And the ruin of that house was great.*
>
> — LUKE 6:46-49 (NKJV)

Believing isn't just mental acceptance or acknowledgement. Everything that we believe dictates our actions and attitude in life. Believing that the brakes will work on your car gives you confidence to increase your speed; believing the laws of motion, though not fully understood, causes you to slow down when approaching a curve on a mountain road. If you've read this book and received some information, that's good; but that's not all. Go and build on the things that we have found in the Word of God. You must do them because you believe them.

We had mentioned that trials and traumas don't change our purpose in life, and I want to bring this to a close by sharing something with you that we have repeated at the church as a body many times over the years. It was a series of statements that we gleaned along the way in our weekly studies in the book of Nehemiah, a book about restoration. Little by little, we added to what we would later call our church manifesto. A manifesto is a written or verbal statement of intentions, and I invite you to adopt this as your own. It goes like this:

> *I am a child of God, destined to make a difference. I will not doubt or fear in the face of adversity. I am committed to God's will for my life no matter what opposition may come. I will praise God for every blessing and through every trial for He will never fail me. I will put God first every day of my life that I may hear Him say: Well done.*

That's true for you, too, and the journey to Dancing with the Scars begins now. God is ready. Are you?